DISCERNING GOD'S WILL TOGETHER
A SPIRITUAL PRACTICE FOR THE CHURCH

DISCERNING GOD'S WILL TOGETHER

A SPIRITUAL PRACTICE FOR THE CHURCH

Danny E. Morris
and
Charles M. Olsen

ALBAN PUBLICATIONS
BETHESDA, MARYLAND

Discerning God's Will Together: A Spiritual Practice for the Church

Published by The Alban Institute by an arrangement with Upper Room Books, 1908 Grand Avenue, P. O. Box 189, Nashville, Tennessee 37202-1890.

Scripture quotations not otherwise identified are from the New Revised Standard Version of the Bible, copyright 1989 by the Division of Christian Education of the National Council of the Churches of Christ in the USA and are used by permission.

Cover Design: Mark Tedeschi
Cover Art: Christ as Good Shepherd. Mosaic: Mausoleum of Galla Placidia,
    Ravenna, Italy/Scala/Art Resource, New York
Interior Design, Art, and Layout: Nancy Cole
First Printing: May 1997
Second Printing: November 1997

The cover art is an ancient mosaic that depicts the sheep as they attempt to discern the voice of their unseen Shepherd.

Library of Congress Cataloging-in-Publication Data

Morris, Danny E.
    Discerning God's will together : a spiritual practice for the church /
        Danny E. Morris and Charles M. Olsen.
        p. cm.
        Includes bibliographical references.
    ISBN 0-8358-0808-4 (paper)
    1. Discernment of spirits. 2. Church group work. 3. God—Will.
    I. Olsen, Charles M. II. Title.
BV5083.M66 1997   96-43229
248—DC20   CIP

Printed in the United States of America

*Dedicated to
all who yearn for and strive to shape
a new kind of church
in which knowing and doing God's will
are ultimate values.*

CONTENTS

INTRODUCTION

A FABLE

The tribe silently moved from the narrow forest path into a beautiful, tree-lined meadow. A small stream ran through the meadow, and green grass formed an inviting carpet on both sides of the stream. Vines of various strengths, textures, and colors hung from the trees that surrounded the meadow.

The tribe had been searching for a path to follow and had seen two openings into the woods, one on each side of the stream. Some members of the tribe wanted to take the path that led through the pine trees; some wanted to take the path through the hardwood. They knew that they needed to stay together, but could not agree on a common path.

When the members of the tribe spied the vines, they began to pick the firmest and strongest; and they began to weave the tendrils into a long rope that would withstand great pressure without breaking.

Then they positioned themselves in two groups, one on each side of the stream, so that they stood closest to the path they favored. Their new rope was stretched across the stream so that everyone would be able to take hold of the rope and pull. A tug-of-war would determine which side would prevail and which path the tribe would follow. "Come over here and pull with us," some called. "We need good strong folks here," came the reply.

The tug-of-war began. At first there was little movement. Then the rope began to move back and forth. First one side was encouraged, then the other side seemed to be winning; and all the while, those on both sides filled the meadow with shouting, panting, groaning. As one group began to prevail, several people from the other side turned loose of the rope and crossed the stream to help them pull. Some nearest the stream slipped on the grass and fell into the mud. Others could not stand the pressure, so they let go of the rope and watched. One group seemed to gain strength and began to pull the rope harder, while their opponents hung on for dear life and hoped, against all odds, to reverse the direction the tug-of-war was taking. Finally, one group was pulled into the narrow stream. The tug-of-war was over.

The people on the winning side happily jumped and danced and cheered, celebrating their triumph. They beckoned to the losers to come join them on their side and to enter their chosen path. Some of the losers slowly fell in place behind the winning group. Others trailed along at a distance. Some were reluctant to join the victors and separated from the tribe. And some trudged up out of the stream, muddy and bruised, and were pulled out and pushed along the new path. The victors marched ahead chanting,

> We are strong.
> We are right.
> We have prevailed
>   with all our might.

After a year or two, the tribe entered a similar meadow. They saw the carpet of grass, a stream that divided the meadow, and the vines hanging from the trees. They noticed two new paths on opposite sides of the meadow. One led through the fruit trees; the other led through the nut trees. Again the members of the tribe were uncertain which path to follow.

However, the tribe had learned from experience. They still picked the vines, but each person chose vines that in some way represented his or her character. Instead of weaving the vines into a single strong rope for a tug-of-war, the members of the tribe fashioned pompoms by holding several vines in each hand.

Then the group began to move back and forth across the stream, exploring the edges of the meadow for new path openings. Paying attention to each person and the colors of his or her pompoms, they began to move in and out, back and forth, up and down, round and round, circling, weaving, whirling. They responded to one another, sometimes deferring to one another, sometimes asserting themselves. A beautiful dance formed and continued until suddenly all at once the tribe ceased its movement. The members of the tribe came to rest with their arms limp and their heads bowed, each savoring the silence.

When they lifted their heads, they found that nearly everyone was standing in a circle on one side of the stream. The sun was rising over a previously unnoticed path in front of them. The few still standing on the other side jumped over the stream and joined the tribe.

With lifted arms, the sage broke the silence. "This is a fine new day. We have found a better way to be a tribe." All the members of the tribe responded by singing,

> When true simplicity is gained,
> To bow and to bend we shan't be ashamed,
> To turn, turn, will be our delight
> 'Till by turning, turning, we come round right.

Then all the members of the tribe proceeded down the path together. Their hymn echoed across the meadow,

> 'Tis the gift to be simple. 'Tis the gift to be free.
> 'Tis the gift to come down where we ought to be,
> And when we find ourselves in the place just right,
> 'Twill be in the valley of love and delight.
> — An Eighteenth-Century Shaker Song

Sometimes groups in the church seek to prevail by using power, influence, reasoned discourse, and carefully plotted strategies. This manual is not about tug-of-war within religious groups. It is about a process like a dance by which a religious group comes to rest on a course of action. In the dance, all of the participants' wisdom and gifts—humility, reason, intuition, tradition, religious practice—are called forth until the divine presence breaks in and lights the right path, offering sight and guidance to individuals and to the group.

THE WAY OF SPIRITUAL DISCERNMENT

Today is an in-between time for the church, between the past, when the church was firmly established in Christendom, and an unclear future for the church. Today is a time for redefinition; it is a time for the church to listen to its stories, to talk about its direction and identity, and to patiently discern the shape of its future life and ministry. Yet people are weary from church business as usual, from church gatherings that do not connect with the deeper meanings of their life and faith. The church must draw on its best traditions of faith and practice in order to find new ways of interacting and deciding. The process of prayerful spiritual discernment draws on the best of the church's practices and offers a depth of faith and life uncommon in the church today.

Current procedures and ways of making decisions in religious groups are limited.

• Reasoned discourse has limitations. We presume that we are smart enough, if we only persevere, to think through fitting solutions to problems and to determine ways of addressing the issues that face us. We reason as a group and come to conclusions that we think are best. Though reasoned discourse is valuable and contributes to spiritual discernment, it all too often becomes a process in which people pool their ignorance, value expediency, enter into political tradeoffs, engage in power plays, and rush to judgment; often the group divides into winners and losers with residual feelings of joy and pain. The process of spiritual discernment draws us beyond our own limited reason to seek divine presence and insight.

• Attempting to obey God's will has limits. Religious groups have had the experience of deciding on a course of action that seemed at the time to be a response to God's will, but did not work out as expected. Errors in judgment often lead to disappointment. People have also been hurt because others, overly zealous for a cause, have imposed their own will in the name of God's will. Because of the way they have made decisions, people in the church may begin to see God's will as unchanging and immovable, like a rock set in a concrete foundation that must be "discovered" and may become a stumbling block. Although the process of spiritual discernment draws on traditions of trying to follow the will of God, it also assumes that we are in an interactive relationship with God and invites us to look to God's heart and to satisfy God's yearnings.

• Individual discernment has limitations. We may be adept at pursuing God's guidance for ourselves. "What is God's will for my life?" we ask. The process of spiritual discernment goes on to ask, "What is God's will for the world? for the church?" These questions include corporate discernment. Spiritual discernment draws on the personal experiences of the saints in all ages of history and translates them for the experience of groups and assemblies today.

• Decision making has its limits. We make decisions. Discernment is given. The Spirit of God, which operates at the deepest levels of the human psyche and within the mysteries of the faith community, brings to the surface gifts of wisdom and guidance, which we only discover and name.

• Ascetic spiritual sight has limits. We stand in awe of the unique spiritual wisdom that some gifted people possess. But when a holy person speaks, dialogue usually ends. He or she has the final word. Discernment as a way of being is shaped by spiritual disciplines: reading the Scriptures, reciting the psalms, and many others. The process of spiritual discernment recognizes the gifts and insights of individuals. It also looks to the wisdom of the whole community as people talk to one another, come to consensus, and take action. Discernment includes both being and doing. It focuses on individuals and communities.

• Procedures and rules have limits. Relying on procedures and rules often becomes rigid and bypasses the importance of community. A community's trust and character do not arise in a vacuum, but only in the context of its moral and religious practices. Spiritual discernment is founded on practices rooted in faith traditions. Alasdair MacIntyre, in *After Virtue*, suggests, "A practice is a coherent and complex form of socially established cooperative human activity which strives to achieve the good."[1]

Practices in faith communities—story telling, confessing, forgiving, blessing, praying, listening, doing acts of mercy, seeking justice and peace, healing, and worshiping—are drawn from tradition and inform the character and process of spiritual discernment.

• Looking for consensus has limits. Coming to consensus may be done in a manner that intimidates quiet people into acquiescence. Time constraints may lead busy people to rush to premature judgments. Many leaders lack experience in how to bring a group to consensus. Some see it as ancient or quaint. Pontius Pilate asked the crowds what should be done with Jesus and gained a quick consensus. God's will is not always found in the consensus. The process of spiritual discernment values consensus not for its own sake, but for the purpose of seeing God's will. Consensus reflects a sense of harmony through interaction—a first step toward corporate discernment. People hoping to discern God's will come to consensus within the framework of spiritual practices. (For over 300 years, Quakers, or Friends, have used practices of spiritual discernment. They have much to teach us about their ways of seeking and listening to God.)

• Parliamentary rules have limits. The church has adopted parliamentary procedures that are useful in large deliberative bodies and provide protection and structure in highly conflicted or impassioned meetings—large or small. Rules of order protect the rights of the minority and assure the will of the majority while also tempering power. But parliamentary procedures are based on an adversarial system that provides a structure for combat. It is a process in which people who are verbal, rational, and extroverted have a decided edge. People who use the process of spiritual discernment appreciate the importance of parliamentary structure as a helpful way of solving problems or addressing issues, but recognize the need for other complementary approaches. If the church has only one approach for conducting meetings, can it receive a vision, respond to an answered prayer, determine the highest calling, or ascertain an ultimate purpose? These will not be decided by popular vote, but will be spiritually discerned.

- Majority rule has limits. A quick vote may shorten a meeting, but does not guarantee that everyone will actively support the decision. In the process of spiritual discernment, the group patiently and prayerfully listens, struggling to see where the Spirit rests, and moves together to a point where everyone can enthusiastically support or at least permit.

- A single way of leading a meeting has limitations. All leaders have benefited from a study of parliamentary rules. High school students have been trained in *Robert's Rules of Order* in Future Farmers of America, on debate teams, or in English classes. But where is the manual for spiritual discernment? The process of spiritual discernment will allow *discernmentarians* to stand beside *parliamentarians*. The person who presides at a meeting can be trained in both disciplines so that she or he will feel comfortable using parliamentary procedure and spiritual discernment either alternately or in conjunction with each other. The process she or he uses will depend on the situation to be addressed. Let him or her be joined by everyone who is weary of routine meetings and hungry for vital spirituality within the church. Let us call with one voice for a new kind of church in which God's business is properly cared for and God's will is properly discerned.

- Business-as-usual meetings have limits. Litanies of committee reports held together by bookend prayers create predictable and sterile meetings. Attending meetings should involve doing worshipful work, which is both the character and method of discernment. In worshipful work, the agenda is detailed to attend to all matters of business appropriate for the body. But more energy is focused on one or two carefully selected matters that call for extensive and deep spiritual discernment. Planned and spontaneous opportunities for worship, such as prayer, song, affirmations of faith, Bible study, story telling, silence, and celebration are woven into the agenda. The meeting becomes a worshipful experience of the presence of the Holy Spirit when participants consciously offer their agenda to God. The place of the meeting becomes holy ground, just as the sanctuary does during worship. The table of the board is not far from the table of the Lord, and the bread of meetings becomes life-giving.

Limiting the church's ways of making decisions creates discordant tones that cannot come together in a hymn, whereas spiritual discernment creates an ode to joy.

SHALL WE ASK THE GOD QUESTIONS?

While doing discernment workshops in various denominations, we are often surprised by the number of people who are afraid of God's will. They fear that if God's will is done, it will result in hardship, that God's will has cutting edges and unhappy results. They fear that God's will may be the worst thing that could happen. Many people fear that God may require them to do almost impossible tasks. If a person asks God to reveal the divine will, he or she may have to quit his or her job, become a missionary, or sell the boat. An uneasy feeling lingers in the church. Don't get too close to God. God will only make life difficult.

If hesitancy to do God's will is as widespread as we observe it to be, then faith communities face a major problem. If individuals and communities block opportunities to seek God's will, they cut themselves off from God and are left to manage with only their own ingenuity, which is all too fallible.

When people seek God's will, their quest leads them to yearn for the will of God, even as God, in love, yearns for them. Yearning may be a softer word than will and may have more meaning for us. God's will and God's yearning are synonymous. God's will is the best thing that can happen to us under any circumstances. Responding to God's yearning produces harmony, not hardship, and power, not problems.

The God questions may well be the most important questions we ask: God, is this your will; yes or no? *What are you guiding us to be or do?*

God meets us at the pivotal points in our lives and in the life of the faith community. Asking the question then has the potential to completely reorient our lives and ministries. Consider:

• How different would your life be if you had frequently and earnestly asked the question, "God, what is your will?"

• What would your church be like if at every important juncture, you and other members of your faith community had consciously asked, "God, what is your will?"

THE AUTHORS' MINISTRIES

Discerning God's Will Together is related to insights from the authors' previous books. In *Yearning to Know God's Will* (Zondervan, 1991), Danny E. Morris presents the ways of discernment in various settings. Aids to discernment can be discovered in the Bible; in the teachings of the faith; and through spiritual intuition, common sense, and guidance by the Holy Spirit. In *Transforming Church Boards into Communities of Spiritual Leaders* (Alban Institute, 1995), Charles M. Olsen presents a four-part model for integrating spirituality and administration at church board or council meetings. The model includes prayerful discernment, story telling, biblical and theological reflection, and vision. *Discerning God's Will Together* introduces helpful ways for individuals and groups to enter into the practice of prayerful spiritual discernment. This book is meant to be used in conjunction with the other two books.

Danny E. Morris is Director of Developing Ministries of The Upper Room, which is a part of The General Board of Discipleship, The United Methodist Church. The Upper Room publishes eight magazines and about thirty books a year.

Danny initiated The New Kind of Church Network of Spiritual Discernment Churches. The original goal of the network was to bring together twenty-five churches of various denominations; the churches would make a covenant to teach and practice the principles of discernment. After fifteen months, more than six hundred churches were participating in the program. Some have chosen to be teaching churches that practice and teach discernment principles. Others have decided to be inquiring churches. They indicate an interest, but have not yet begun to practice discernment. They learn of the experience of the teaching churches. The *New Kind of Church* newsletter is a quarterly publication written primarily by the teaching churches and sent to both groups. For more information about the network, write to Danny E. Morris, The Upper Room, Box 189, Nashville, TN 37202-0189.

Charles M. (Chuck) Olsen is Program Director at the Heartland Presbyterian Center, where he is the staff mentor for Worshipful-Work: Center for Transforming Religious Leadership. Worshipful-Work is an outgrowth of a Lilly Endowment project in church board development. Over a four-year period, a model was developed that integrated administration and spirituality in church governance. Based at the Heartland Presbyterian Center, the project is ecumenical in scope. Worshipful-Work offers resources, consultation, seminars, and retreats in spiritual formation for lay and clergy leaders of congregations and religious associations. For more information, contact Chuck Olsen at Worshipful-Work, 16965 NW 45 Hwy., Kansas City, MO 64152.

INTRODUCTION TO THE CHAPTERS

1. Discernment: What?

Discernment creates the capacity to see. To discern is to see through to the essence of a matter. Discernment distinguishes the real from the phony, the true from the false, the good from the evil, and the path toward God from the path away from God. Spiritual discernment sees reality from God's perspective. It is sight from the outside in; discernment penetrates the inner nature of things. It is also sight from the inside out by people who know intuitively.

At its best, discernment operates in the context of vision. Within the context of seeing the whole landscape, or forest, discernment sees the shape and character of the particular tree. Within the context of the church's vision, the kingdom of God, discernment sees God's yearning in and for a particular situation.

Discernment also operates in the context of commitment. It

prompts a particular response, and individuals and communities make a commitment and are prepared to act decisively.

Scripture and the experience of the church offer a rich treasure from which to form our contemporary practices of spiritual discernment.

2. Discernment: Why?

As people of faith, we believe that God is alive and active in the world of human experience. Desiring to participate in God's activity, we look for God's guidance and listen for God's call. Many other voices from the surrounding culture beckon to us, holding the promise of fulfillment, meaning, and satisfaction. Those voices speak both from within ourselves and from the outside world. As a result, we try to discern the various voices, or spirits; then put them to the test: Are they true or false? good or evil? Like the gold miner, we test for real gold.

3. Discernment: Who?

Discernment is personal, but never entirely private. It engages the person in the depths of his or her soul and therefore in a profound relationship with the Spirit of God. Discernment also involves the person in the community of faith and brings the community to decisions that order its life and ministry. Spiritual discernment draws both the individual and the community into the world.

4. Discernment: How?

We are not responsible for reinventing the discernment wheel. Saints through the ages have practiced discernment, and we need to listen to them. We also need to recognize how vulnerable we are to the ways the world makes decisions and directs our lives.

The process of discernment is not mechanical. Though we suggest a process, it is not "ten easy steps" to spiritually fulfilling decisions. Discernment does not insure that if we approach a matter in a particular way, we will generate a desired outcome.

Who can fathom the mind and will of God, anyway? What presumption! In spiritual discernment, we draw on time-honored practices and disciplines of faith and rely on them as we step forth onto holy ground and into mystery.

5. Discernment: Where?

Discernment takes place in the "closet" of personal solitude. There, like monsters in a closet, ego and the need for personal glory may raise their ugly heads. (Jesus was tempted by power, pride, and possessions in exchange for his God-centered soul.) Discernment also takes place in the familiarity of the "house" or small group. In prayer, confession, honesty, creative imagination, and probing scrutiny, clear direction emerges. Discernment also takes place in the "sanctuary," in large, deliberative assemblies.

These biblical metaphors are set forth in Acts 2:46 and Matthew 6:6. The "closet," "house," and "sanctuary" are connected; each one affects the others. Together they are the places where people come to the wisdom of spiritual discernment. Every aspect of church systems can be both a source and a beneficiary of these practices.

DISCERNMENT: WHAT?

DEFINITIONS

To discern means

- to separate or distinguish (from the Latin *discernere*);
- to test in crisis or to distinguish good and evil (from the Greek *diakrisis*);
- to find the authentic and valuable and to recognize the counterfeit (like biting a coin to see if it is gold);
- to see to the heart of the matter with spiritual eyes; from God's vantage point, to see beneath the surface of events, through illusions within human systems, and beyond the immediate and transient;
- to locate the immediate and particular within a vision of the broad and distant landscape (to see the trees in the forest);
- to possess immediate and direct insight.

"Spiritual discernment makes operational our faith that an ever present Guide . . . is present to lead us in the way of truth and love as individuals and congregations. It opens our sails as a church to the Spirit whose winds we believe are always blowing and will always move us closer to Christ, closer to one another, and closer to the world that God wills."[1]

BIBLICAL CITINGS OF DISCERNMENT

Israel's symbols of God's presence—the burning bush, a pillar of fire by night and a cloud by day—attested to God's investment in and commitment to human beings. Dreams, angels, and the "sound of sheer silence" affirmed the mystery of God. Practical observations of the fate of the righteous and the unrighteous became a body of wisdom used to instruct the young.

In the Hebrew Scriptures, discernment is mentioned only once; in 1 Kings 3:9, Solomon asks, "Give your servant therefore an understanding mind to govern your people, able to discern between good and evil." (Many verses equate discernment with deciding and understanding.) The Old Testament includes marvelous, dramatic stories of people who sought God's will above all else. The prophets, if they were not false prophets, were first-rate discerners of the divine will. They were the seers of Israel; they saw from the divine perspective. The prophets saw the big picture, Israel's vision of *shalom*, in which God would reign and neighbors would be at peace. Without spiritual discernment, the prophets would have been silent; they spoke what they discerned.

God chose people to be agents of discernment. Elders, who were wise and who discerned the wisdom of God, sat at the gates of passage and commerce and made God's ways known to the community. Schools of prophets grew out of the charisma of particularly gifted and insightful people. Often their simple and austere spirituality validated their calling and freed them to speak to the powerfully elite while advocating justice for the poor. National rulers had court-appointed, in-house prophets who could discern God's will and provide counsel in political, economic, and military matters.

Discernment engages hearing. Elijah stood in the entrance to a cave and felt the earth shake and saw the lightning flash and finally, in the "sound of sheer silence" (1 Kings 19:12), heard the voice of God. Discernment didn't come in the display of God's pyrotechnics, but in the hearing of a voice.

Discernment engages sight. God sent Samuel to select one of Jesse's sons to be king. When he saw Eliab, he thought, "Surely the Lord's anointed is now before the Lord." But God told Samuel not to rely on appearances: "The Lord does not see as mortals see, they look on the outward appearance, but the Lord looks on the heart" (1 Samuel 16:6-7). He looked over seven sons and could find no king among them. Then young David was brought in from tending the sheep; and Samuel recognized the heart of David, a future king.

Discernment engages speech. Moses was not eloquent, but God gave Aaron his brother to speak for him. And God said to Moses, "You shall speak to him and put the words in his mouth; and I will be with your mouth and with his mouth, and will teach you what you shall do. He indeed shall speak for you to the people; he shall serve as a mouth for you, and you shall serve as God for him" (Exodus 4:15-16).

Discernment recognizes the presence of God. Jacob wrestled all night with an emissary of the Lord. When morning came, Jacob, who was slow to discern, said, "'Please tell me your name.' But he said, 'Why is it that you ask my name?' And there he blessed him" (Genesis 32:29).

Discernment is distinguishing good from evil. Solomon asked for "an understanding mind...to discern between good and evil"; and God gave Solomon a "wise and discerning mind" (1 Kings 3:9-12).

In the New Testament, discernment is mentioned directly in the following verses:

• Romans 12:2: "Be transformed by the renewing of your minds, so that you may discern what is the will of God—what is good and acceptable and perfect."

• 1 Corinthians 12:10: God gives the gift of "discernment between spirits."

- 1 John 4:1: "Do not believe every spirit, but test [discern] the spirits to see whether they are from God."
- Ephesians 1:18: "I pray that the God of our Lord Jesus Christ, may give you a spirit of wisdom and revelation as you come to know him, so that, with the eyes of your heart enlightened, you may know what is the hope to which he has called you."

The New Testament also tells about people who, as the usual focus of their lives, discerned the will of God.

Mary yearned for deeper wisdom about her son. Joseph eventually discerned God's will and dared to think about Mary in a new way (Matthew 1:19-25). For Elizabeth, Mary's cousin, discernment of God's will seemed to come naturally (see Luke 1:36-45).

Jesus discerned the heart of God. He was named God's beloved son, and his baptism provided a foundation from which to discern the spirits. When he was driven into the wilderness to be tempted, he saw through illusions of power, fame, and possessions and chose servanthood, humility, and poverty. Seeing clearly the kingdom of God, Jesus told stories that cut to the heart of human self-deception, illusion, and desire. Jesus was a sage, embodying the heritage of the wisdom tradition. His passion and faithfulness presented a criterion for discernment and offered good news for the poor and sinful. From his baptism—when a voice from heaven announced, "This is my Son, the Beloved, with whom I am well pleased" (Matthew 3:17)—throughout his ministry—until his death and his final cry "It is finished" (John 19:30)—Jesus' life bespoke a total commitment to discerning and doing God's will.

The apostles discerned God's will and proclaimed the good news about Jesus Christ. Peter discerned God's call to go to Macedonia (Acts 16:9-10). Paul, on the way to Damascus, heard God's word (Acts 9:1-22) and discerned God's will for his life. Young Stephen discerned a reality that others did not see, and he had a unique relationship with God (see especially Acts 7:59-60).

Let us not forget First Church, Jerusalem. The book of Acts records four occasions when the church sought to discern God's will (see Acts 1:12-26; 6:1-7; 11:1-18; and 15). Members of the New Testament church believed that God would guide individuals and communities; they expected to be led by the Spirit (see Galatians 5:18, Romans 8:14). Their relationship with God, their awareness of the presence and gifts of the Spirit, their practice of prayer, their reception and proclamation of the good news, and their infectious love of the community present a convincing picture of a way of life with discernment at its core.

Early Christians feared the voices of false prophets, so they tested the spirits. Only the presence of the Spirit of God would determine what served the common good of the community and would offer the love and knowledge to provide the community with authentic spiritual leadership. "We have received not the spirit of the world, but the Spirit that is from God, so that we may understand the gifts bestowed on us by God. And we speak of these things in words not taught by human wisdom but taught by the Spirit, interpreting spiritual things to those who are spiritual" (1 Corinthians 2:12-13).

When the church in Jerusalem heard that Christians were arguing about whether converts should be circumcised, the apostles and elders met to consider the question. They came to one mind and heart through discernment (read Acts 15). The church never decided to discern God's will. Discernment seemed to come as a gift; the apostles and elders knew what to do. The early church used the language of discernment: "Then the apostles and the elders, with the consent of the whole church, decided . . ." (Acts 15:22) or "It seemed good to the apostles and elders, with the whole church . . ." (NRSV). Paul and Barnabas were sent to Antioch with a letter that said, "We have decided unanimously to choose representatives and send them to you" (verse 25). Again, the letter reads, "For it has seemed good to the Holy Spirit and to us to impose on you no further burden than these essentials" (Acts 15:28-29). All of this is the language of discernment.

When the delegation arrived in Antioch, they assembled the congregation and delivered the letter sent from Jerusalem. "When its members read it, they rejoiced at the exhortation" (verse 31). The discernment of the apostles and elders was worked out in the congregation. The right and happy result was that God's will on a difficult issue had been clearly discerned.

Discernment is deeply rooted in both the Old and New Testaments. In the Jerusalem church, discernment naturally moved out of the biblical record and into the church.

HISTORY

The practice of discernment has roots in the Judeo-Christian tradition. Human awareness of the presence of God prompts questions: God, what are you up to in the world? What is my part in it? The conviction that divine guidance operates in the human world invites us into a process of discernment.

Discernment was developed in the practice of the early church fathers and mothers and worked out in the experience of the faithful. In the 1600s, St. Ignatius put forth the now classical "Spiritual Exercises" on discernment. What emphases on discernment were occurring after the Jerusalem church in Acts 15 and before Ignatius presented the Spiritual Exercises? The tradition of discernment is remarkable.

Origen, in the third century, saw human thoughts coming from three sources: God, evil spirits, and good spirits. If people could trace their thoughts (discern the spirits), they could find a way to give themselves to the proper spirit, for people are moved by the spirits to good or evil.[2]

John Cassian, in the fourth century, followed Origen's lead. His twenty-four *Conferences* presented a study of the Egyptian ideal of a monk. The subject of the second conference was discernment. He saw three sources of thought: God (illumination of Holy Spirit), the devil (who makes sin attractive), and ourselves (thoughts of what we have done or heard). "We must therefore keep a close eye on this threefold scheme of our thoughts and we must exercise wise discretion concerning them as they surface in our hearts. Right from the beginning, we will scrutinize their origins and their causes, deciding our necessary reaction to them in the light of who it is that suggests them."[3]

Cassian said that discernment is the eye and lamp of the body; he referred to the biblical image of the sound eye that produces light for the body and the diseased eye that makes darkness. The monk who discerns:

• is kept from veering to the left in carelessness and sin, sluggishness of spirit, and pretext of control;

• is kept from veering to the right in stupid presumption and excessive fervor beyond restraint.[4]

Cassian also offered the image of the test applied by the money-changer who discerned true gold. We are to place thoughts on the scales of our heart and weigh them with exacting care. "1) Is it filled with what is good for all? 2) Is it heavy with the fear of God? 3) Is it genuine in the feelings which underlie it? 4) Is it lightweight because of human show or because of some thrust toward novelty? 5) Has the burden of vainglory lessened its merit or diminished its luster?" (1:21)[5]

For Cassian, humility was the path for the search. A monk was to openly disclose his thoughts to his spiritual guide. Self-disclosure and obedience, which produces humility, leads to discernment.

John Climacus, in the sixth century, had great respect for the insights of Cassian. Climacus was selected to be the abbott at Sinai after living for years as a hermit in the desert. In an effort to be a wise abbott, he wrote *The Ladder of Divine Ascent*, presenting thirty steps for monks to consider. Step number twenty-six is on discernment. He cites Cassian's work on discernment, which he calls a "beautiful and sublime" philosophy: "From humility comes discernment, from discernment comes insight, and from insight comes foresight. And who would not run this fine race of obedience when such blessings are there ahead of him?"[6] The steps in Climacus' ladder were arranged in juxtaposition to one another. We should not be surprised to see that number four, "Obedience," was matched with number twenty-six, "Discernment."

In *Ladder of Divine Ascent*, Climacus presents three progressive stages of discernment. For beginners it is self-understanding; for intermediates, the spiritual capacity to distinguish the good from what is opposed to it; for the advanced, direct God-given light, which affects people and the world around them.[7]

The focus of discernment in the early church remained on individuals and on interpersonal relationships. Sensitivity to communal discernment had not yet been developed.

The church in the east and the church in the west developed different patterns of wisdom in discernment and decision making.

The eastern church looked to the wisdom of mystics and ascetics. Bishops sought communal wisdom for the good of the community. Desert fathers and mothers returned to villages where people looked to them for wisdom. The *Philokalia* (1782) pulled together important sources on discernment, from the fourth to the fifteenth centuries, which would guide the pilgrim in the spiritual life.[8] When God spoke through a spiritual ascetic, debate ended; the ascetic's capacity to sway others was enormous because discernment was viewed as a gift of God.

Because of their emphasis on the Holy Spirit, the Orthodox churches offer us a unique gift: an understanding of experience through trinitarian structures. The Orthodox see in threes, discerning the presence of God beyond, with, and in experience.

The western church adapted itself to the patterns of the Roman Empire. Early on, Roman law and styles of deliberation were introduced in the church. The great councils of the western church had their roots in the Roman senate, a deliberative body. As the senate debated issues of state, the church argued over issues of doctrine. Participants stood one at a time and presented their arguments, citing authorities who would support them. Then members of the council voted to agree, disagree, or abstain.

The Roman Catholic Church was hierarchical. Cardinals, the great princes of the church, were primary authority figures. The unity of the church was grounded in the authority of the pope. In the western church, discernment was focused by the importance of authority, tradition, unity, and continuity.

Even the monasteries reflected the decision-making patterns of the church in Rome, but with some adaptations. Each monastery had a chapter room where discussion and debate took place. The abbot or abbess may or may not have made final decisions, but the wisdom of the community played a significant role. For Saint Benedict, for instance, the "narrow way" meant walking in another's discretion and wisdom.

The Dark Ages cast more light on discernment than we are prone to admit. In addition to monastic expressions of faithfulness, the piety of the common people found expression in the mystics of the period. Meister Eckhart and the Friends of God embraced a practical piety that people could understand. Thomas à Kempis, in *Of the Imitation of Christ*, presented a practical style of discernment that centered on following Christ.[9]

The dawning of the Renaissance took place in the century between the two great councils of the Roman Catholic Church. In the Council of Constance (1415–1418), the powers of the state were present and the schism of the papacy ended. In the Council of Trent (1545–1563), Catholic dogma was formalized in reaction to Protestant tenets of faith, which were considered anathema. The Roman Church defined the authority of Scripture in relationship to tradition and the authority of the pope. Reform, which could have drawn on the practices of discernment, was not included in the agenda of either meeting.

One of the most dynamic centuries in history appeared between these two bookend councils.

During the Council of Constance, John Huss was burned at the stake for invoking the authority of the Bible for discernment. He was the spiritual father of what we know as the Moravian Church.

Ignatius of Loyola, the founder of the Jesuits, in *Spiritual Exercises*, outlined "Rules for Discernment of Spirits."[10] The list of rules was extensive and unique. Though many of the rules were drawn from time-honored traditions of discernment, others were new. The rules included the importance of imagination, reason, biblical connections, experience, testing the spirits, and feelings. The affective influences were central. People involved in spiritual discernment put matters to the test—resting them in the heart, looking for consolation, which leads toward God in peace, or desolation, which leads away from God in distress. Rules for discernment of spirits were applied primarily to matters of individual discernment, but could be expanded for the purposes of communal discernment.

The writings of the mystics, John of the Cross and Teresa of Avila, presented another dimension to the process of discernment by introducing the aspect of human desire. Our deepest longings and desires are for God. All other desires are stripped, sometimes painfully, as we find true satisfaction in God and in doing God's will.

In the Protestant Reformation, Luther, Calvin, and Zwingli brought forth the evangelical principles of grace alone through faith and the centrality of Scripture. Scripture was seen as the divine spectacles through which one could discern God's leading.

The Protestant Reformation, and influence of John Calvin, in particular, with his emphasis on decency and order, planted seeds that eventually grew in the parliamentary culture in England. Calvin, who found himself in a chaotic setting in Geneva, tried to bring about both order and piety while fashioning Geneva into a city of God. A reading of his *Institutes of the Christian Religion* reveals how western his thinking was.[11] Without question, he bought into the Greek and Roman methods of rational debate. The voting practices of the Swiss Cantons were followed in the church. Indeed, he stretched the meaning of Acts 14, in which Paul and Barnabas appointed elders, to suggest that the people voted on the appointments with a show of hands.

Calvin was a lawyer by training, relying on rules and ordinances to insure that everything was done decently and in order. Calvin both contributes to and limits our inquiry into discernment by placing emphasis on:

• the importance of church government. "Each church, therefore, had from its beginning a Senate, chosen from godly, grave, and holy men, which had jurisdiction over the correcting of faults. This office of government is necessary for all ages."[12]

• the importance of God's calling those who lead and decide. "In order that noisy and troublesome men should not rashly take upon themselves to teach or to rule, especial care was taken that no one should assume public office in the church without being called."[13]

• the place and importance of Christ as the actual presider. "Now it is Christ's right to preside over all councils and to have no man share his dignity. But I say that he presides only when the whole assembly is governed by his word and Spirit."[14]

"If one seeks in Scripture what the authority of councils is, there exists no clearer promise than in this statement of Christ's: 'Where two or three are gathered together in my name, there I am in the midst of them' (Matt.18:20). But that nonetheless refers as much to a little meeting as to a universal council. Christ will be in the midst of a council only if it is gathered together in his name. I deny that they are gathered in his name who, casting aside God, ordain anything according to their own decision; who, not content with the oracles of Scripture, concoct some novelty out of their own heads."[15]

• the importance of reason. "The same thing happened to them [councils] that Roman senators of old themselves complained of—senatorial decrees were badly framed. For so long as opinions are counted, not weighed, the better part had often to be overcome by the greater."[16]

• the importance of organization, structure, form, and law to bind us together. "We see that some form of organization is necessary in all human society to foster the common peace and maintain concord." Therefore, if we wish to provide for the safety of the church, we must attend with all diligence to Paul's command that "all things be done decently and in order" (1 Cor. 14:40).

"Yet since such diversity exists in the customs of men, such variety in their minds, such conflicts in their judgments and dispositions, no organization is sufficiently strong unless constituted with definite laws; nor can any procedure be maintained without some set form. (Nor can Paul's requirement—that 'all things be done decently and in order'—be met unless order itself and decorum be established through the addition of observances that form, as it were, a bond of union."[17]

• the danger of spirituality. Calvin held a basic distrust of the ascetic. This created a division, a split between spirituality and administration. "But in these observances one thing must be guarded against. They are not to be considered necessary for salvation and thus bind consciences by scruples; nor are they to be associated with the worship of God, and piety thus be lodged in them."[18]

As much as the fathers of the early church speak of it, discernment did not appear in Calvin's vocabulary. He rightly feared that devotion to the observances could create a kind of salvation system. (Note the devotion and passion with which some people participate in parliamentary process.) But he also erroneously feared associating the observances, or practices, of communal discernment with worship, lest worship be contaminated. Neither did he want to associate piety (spirituality) with church governance because spirituality moves into an area that is beyond the control of reason. Calvin did not demonstrate any practical awareness that the same Hebrew words are used for worship and work. He would have difficulty with a model of worshipful-work. The separation of governance and administration from spirituality—which is the malady of many church boards, councils, and assemblies today—is therefore solidly rooted in the Reformation!

The Anabaptists tried to model their churches on the New Testament church. They involved the whole faith community in decision making. Because of persecutions, Anabaptists were left with a deep distrust of the state and felt that too many churches had compromised discernment by cooperating with the powers of the state.

Following the Reformation, the seventeenth- and eighteenth-century Quakers made noteworthy contributions to the practice of discernment. They looked to the presence of the Spirit to provide guidance, listened to the promptings of the Spirit in the gathered community, and followed the Spirit's lead. Listening in silence fostered the intuitive capacity of the community of Friends.

The communal character of Friends' understanding and practice of discernment was evident from their beginning and is still the character of Quaker meetings today.

In addition, the Friends brought to discernment the practices of coming to a consensus, the clearness committee, making a minute, and registering non-concurrence.

In the Methodist tradition, discernment has played a role in the spiritual growth of individuals and communities. The Methodist movement created for spiritual nurture and guidance three types of small groups: classes, bands, and the select band.

The class was a small group of people who sought a personal relationship with God. The class leader was appointed by the Wesleys or their assistants and was a person with common sense, an experience of saving grace, and the ability to interpret the Bible to the members of the class. Each week, the leader would inquire about the spiritual state of class members, then offer prayer and guidance suited to the needs expressed by individuals. Spiritual discernment came through interaction with the class leader, who asked questions that led people to think about and to listen for what the Spirit intended for their lives.

The Methodist bands were for people who had experienced new birth or saving faith. While the focus of spiritual formation in the class meeting was "to flee from the wrath to come" and "to watch over one another in love," the focus of the band meeting was to deepen the participants' discipleship through obedience to the scriptural command to "confess your sins to one another, and pray for one another, so that you may be healed" (James 5:16). Members of the bands and the select bands were accountable to one another, and the will of God was discerned through dialogue, prayer, and experimentation.[19]

The select society or select band provided guidance and support for people who had either the desire or the experience of perfect love: love of God with all one's heart, soul, strength, and mind. All members of the select band (including the Wesleys) were peers. There were no membership restrictions based upon gender or marital status. The group's focus was on understanding and experiencing perfect love toward God and neighbor. Spiritual discernment was found in the interaction of group members.

In Puritan New England, during the eighteenth century, Jonathan Edwards was concerned about the excesses of the Great Awakening in which he participated. He wanted to provide people with a way of processing their experiences. In particular, he wanted to help pastors deal with members of their congregations who had been awakened. Believing that most experiences of the Great Awakening were valid, he sought to help people look for signs that would separate the wheat from the chaff and identify experiences that were genuine.

In England, the political advent of rule by law and parliamentary procedure had a powerful impact on the church. The Church of Scotland was run by parliamentary rules. In fact, when the powers of state were consolidated in London, the General Assembly of the Presbyterian Church in Scotland took over administration of the city of Edinburgh. Scottish leaders who had practiced and refined parliamentary order in Scotland made their presence felt in the Royal Parliament. When the Presbyterian Church in America was embroiled in new school/old school controversies, it needed procedures by which to conduct meetings. The Scots readily provided the manual.

Church history shows that discernment in Europe was made by a body of elite equals, but the parliaments and town meetings that cropped up in every village in America led the church to embrace a culture of argument and persuasion. From about 1820, many churches adopted a faith that common people would discern the truth if they had the facts. The church's theology of sin and evil fit in with democracy; government by the people would hold in check the evil intentions of a few.

As denominations developed in the United States, rules and

procedures for church assemblies gradually became standardized. In 1871, the General Assembly of the Presbyterian Church sent a short set of general rules to the presbyteries. The rules were uniform, so there would be no regional variation.

Prior to this, an officer in the United States Army, Henry Martyn Robert, had given thought to the deliberations of religious assemblies. He had been frustrated by the inept ways that meetings were conducted in his American Baptist church. When asked to preside over a church meeting in 1863, he drafted a brief statement of rules of order based on Thomas Jefferson's rules for the United States Congress. The experience prompted him to expand on the effort, producing what we know as *Robert's Rules of Order*.[20] General Robert wanted to standardize them for use in various religious and civic settings so that people would be familiar with a consistent method of making decisions. The effort was calculated to show that the ways religious bodies make decisions is no different from the way other organizations make decisions. Robert's rules have been widely used in the church. But they are designed as rules for combat useful in any arbitration.[21]

Historian Michael Cartright points out several other interesting developments that occurred at the same time *Robert's Rules of Order* was written. Francis Lieber wrote *General Orders 100* on the rules of conduct in war. The methods of fighting created so many casualties (note the casualties in the Civil War) that rules were offered to limit casualties and to make war more humane. Lieber's rules of combat in war have significance for the concept of just war and for restraint in modern wars.

Cartright also related that a friend of his had been appointed pastor of a church in the Baltimore-Washington Conference. On her arrival at the church, she learned that the two previous administrative council meetings had come to an end when council members started throwing chairs at one another. Everyone felt that a significant transition had been made when the first meeting of the council during her pastorate ended without violence. In that case, *Robert's Rules of Order* actually did limit combat!

The rules of order are helpful in handling different points of view on designated subjects. The rules are most helpful in highly charged situations and with large groups; although some of the principles—considering one matter at a time, protecting the rights of the minority, assuring the will of the majority—are important, the rules cannot, in and of themselves, provide the structure for spiritual discernment.

Recent developments in leadership theory, not-for-profit board development, and conflict resolution have influenced church administration. Coupled with a resurgence of interest in spirituality and general dissatisfaction with the present operation of church boards and assemblies, they have led to greater interest in the practice of discernment, both personal and communal. The church can now draw on its traditions of spiritual discernment and order its life and ministries according to the will of God.

SOME BASIC ASSUMPTIONS
ABOUT SPIRITUAL DISCERNMENT

Presence

1. We assume that God is self-disclosing and that God yearns for the created world and enters into a covenant relationship with God's people.

2. We assume that God enters into human existence with such vulnerability that people, in discerning the higher purpose of the divine will, are drawn into the vulnerability of God.

3. We assume that the indwelling Holy Spirit is the active and ongoing guide in personal and corporate discernment.

Practices

4. We assume that seeking God's will is the ultimate value in our knowledge and experience.

5. We assume the need to participate humbly in a faith community of grace.

6. We assume that people and communities need to patiently persevere in practices related to Scripture, prayer, and discernment until God's leading is known.

Posture

7. We assume that the willingness to change the heart and to make an appropriate response are preconditions of the gift of discernment.

8. We assume that God uses especially gifted people with skills and insight into the discernment process in the ministry of discernment.

9. We assume that the practice of discernment is ongoing—to discern God's will again and again and again.

COMMENTARY ON THE BASIC ASSUMPTIONS ABOUT SPIRITUAL DISCERNMENT

Presence

1. *We assume that God is self-disclosing and that God yearns for the created world and enters into a covenant relationship with God's people.*

The God whose will we endeavor to discern is neither detached nor aloof. God's yearning for relationship is affirmed throughout Scripture. There is no secret about who God is (God is Creator) or what God continues to do (God yearns for the created world and for a relationship with God's people).

God offers more than a token agreement or even a binding contract; God offers a covenantal relationship. That fact vouches for God's monumental self-disclosure. Even if the covenant that God offers is rejected, God still yearns for a relationship with God's people.

In discernment, we are given the opportunity to know the divine will, to see God who is self-disclosing and who is forever committed to having a covenantal relationship with God's people.

2. *We assume that God enters into human existence with such vulnerability that people, in discerning the higher purpose of the divine will, are drawn into the vulnerability of God.*

God became incarnate in Jesus because God was willing to be humble and to become obedient to the power and focus of the divine creation. (Think of it!) Discernment means becoming vulnerable to other people and to God. Human pretense and the spirit of covetousness have to go. Protecting our turf and accommodating only ourselves will not do. Let openness come forth!

To be vulnerable is to be open to other people and to God, and it means taking risks. Discernment requires us to be vulnerable because God's will cannot be shaped or manipulated by human beings. We are vulnerable when confronted by the divine because God has been ultimately vulnerable through God's incarnation in Jesus. Vulnerability like we find in Jesus may be what moves us to discern the will of God.

3. *We assume that the indwelling Holy Spirit is the active and ongoing guide in personal and corporate discernment.*

Techniques, discernment principles, and skill in particular disciplines do not give us the power of discernment, but the Holy Spirit does. The Holy Spirit initiates discernment. Then techniques, principles, and skills may be helpful. Spiritual discernment is more than a human endeavor, a set of slick principles, an intervention strategy, or a fix-it remedy to correct or head off problems in the church, it is a profoundly spiritual experience that requires individuals or communities to be profoundly spiritual. Since the indwelling Holy Spirit makes discernment possible, the Holy Spirit initially puts in place the human yearning to discern the divine will. The Holy Spirit enables and guides the process of discernment through rocky ground and rough waters and keeps us from getting tangled up in other motivations for deciding and acting. The Holy Spirit shows us the way by radiating the light of truth and the presence of God's unspoiled will. The Holy Spirit shines divine light on the faces and hearts of people and communities so they can discern God's will.

In discernment, we assume the presence and active involvement of the Holy Spirit. People hoping to discern the yearnings of God will be sensitive to the presence, the initiatives, and the movement of the Spirit because without the Holy Spirit's involvement, there can be no spiritual discernment. The question is, Do we trust the Holy Spirit to be our guide?

Like an archaeologist, the Spirit works within us to uncover the wisdom and discernment buried deep within ourselves. The Spirit, who has planted a leading within us, brings it to the surface of conscious awareness.

Practices

4. *We assume that seeking God's will is the ultimate value in our knowledge and experience.*

God's will is obviously a higher value than the other values that motivate us: efficiency, expediency, unity at any cost, ego, politics, economics, charity, or concern about what other people think.

We hold dear and, often unwittingly, protect our motivations; but can we surrender them so that we can be open to God's will? Everyone who hopes to discern the will of God asks a similar question: Am I able to give up my will for the sake of discerning God's will?

Clearly focusing on God's will as the ultimate value is necessary to the process of personal discernment. It is even more important when people engage in corporate discernment. Even one person can weaken or derail spiritual discernment if he or she holds on to motivations other than the ultimate one of knowing God's will.

5. *We assume the need to participate humbly in a faith community of grace.*

A Christian community is essential for discernment. The community may be represented by one person who is part of the larger Christian community and brings its faith and values to a particular situation. Or several people may be a community that will focus on the needs of one person by his or her invitation. No one should attempt spiritual discernment by himself or herself without putting decisions to the test of other spiritual friends.

In corporate discernment, the Christian community involves itself in complex ways:

• Many people are involved in discerning God's will related to a single issue.

• They may have a variety of opinions and motivations.

• They may have different time constraints, and the community may have additional time requirements.

• They bring to the group psychological, theological, historical, and emotional differences.

In the church, it is often a board, council, committee, or work group that is given the opportunity and challenge of discerning God's will for God's people.

If discernment of God's will is not pursued in the faith community, the church will be left with secondary motivations (efficiency, expediency, politics) for decision and action.

Whether discernment is personal or corporate, Christian community cannot be ignored. The Christian community understands that spiritual discernment requires a special calling and commitment.

6. *We assume that people and communities need to patiently persevere in practices related to Scripture, prayer, and discernment until God's leading is known.*

Discernment is not a quick fix for spiritual damage or a way to bail out a person, a group, or a situation. It is not a clever way to get people to agree. And it is not desirable simply because it is *spiritual* discernment.

Let us acknowledge the truth about our history and admit that it has often been devoid of spiritual discernment. We will require patience and perseverance to take even one step toward discernment and fortitude to continue until we have a sense of commitment and a smattering of experience and knowledge.

The habit and the practices of discernment may aid our understanding.

If we habitually practice the spiritual disciplines, our souls will find a focus and foundation. Then spirituality becomes for us a way of being.

The practices of discernment may also be helpful. There are proven principles that aid the discernment process. To ignore them is to settle for lesser motivations and outcomes.

As important as the practices of discernment are, it would be improper to list them before the habit of discernment, because if the Holy Spirit has not been welcomed into the life of the discerner, practices of discernment will be empty and impotent. The habit of discernment constitutes a way of being, by which we are steeped in spirituality as a way of life; and spirituality becomes as necessary as the air we breathe. The habit of spirituality precedes the practices of discernment.

Not practicing discernment in the church is unthinkable. Without spiritual discernment, we still have to be patient and persevere, which are essentials for discernment. Without discernment we also have no hope of a new kind of church in which God's will is valued above all else.

Posture

7. *We assume that the willingness to change the heart and to make an appropriate response are preconditions to the gift of discernment.*

Perhaps all of the basic assumptions of spiritual discernment come down to this one. Once we have received the gift of discernment, once we feel that we know God's will in a particular situation, are we willing to make the appropriate response? Or will we walk away?

An appropriate response and our willingness to make an appropriate response are not one and the same. Our ability and willingness to be vulnerable and open will more than likely determine whether spiritual discernment will bring about a change of heart.

The question of willingness must be answered before the process of discernment begins: Are we willing to do God's will even before we know it? Or do we prefer to play games with God: "God, show me your will; and if I like it, I will do it." Spiritual discernment is not a game, and playing games with God leads to nothing but frustration. So the question stands, Are we willing to do God's will? If our answer is yes, what is an appropriate response? When we have properly discerned God's will, we will know the proper response.

8. *We assume that God uses especially gifted people with skills and insight into the discernment process in the ministry of discernment.*

God promises that leaders will emerge within the community and that they will have gifts that have been bestowed for the upbuilding and health of the community. Discernment of spirits is a gift.

Business management, education, athletics, and the arts all recognize particularly gifted people. The parliaments of the world find the skills of parliamentarians helpful in decision making. Surely, the people of God, who are called to follow God's guidance, will benefit from people who have been graced by God and who have had opportunities to probe the depths and nuances of the practices of discernment.

Particularly gifted people do not appoint themselves to the ministry of spiritual discernment. Their ministry is initiated by the call of God and validated by the community. Self-awareness, the prompting of the Spirit, and the confirmation of the community bring people to the ministry of discernment.

9. *We assume that the practice of discernment is ongoing—we discern God's will again and again and again.*

Spiritual discernment for an individual or for the larger Christian community is not an occasional exercise. The person or group will want to know God's will on every substantive issue.

Therefore, the question keeps arising: Is this God's will?

Not every situation raises an issue of discernment. God is not likely to be concerned with whether someone drives the brown car or the white car to work. Some items (approving the minutes, receiving a report) that come before the group are not issues for discernment. However, there are times (more often than we honor) when God's will should be known and a response taken. Deciding whether an issue is a matter for discernment is itself a matter for discernment.

Let us habitually keep in mind and heart the discernment question, Does God have anything to do with this situation or issue? If the answer is yes, then it is a matter for discernment.

Ask the question again and again and again and again and again. The goal is to make discernment a pattern, a way of life, so that individuals and congregations can begin to discern the unspoiled will of God.

2

DISCERNMENT: WHY?

THE PURPOSE AND GOAL
OF DISCERNMENT

The purpose and goal of spiritual discernment is knowing and doing God's will. We can easily become enamored with discernment definitions, strategies for holding meetings, the emotional rush of doing something new, or even the self-adulation for attempting to do something spiritual. The newness of our endeavor may compromise our vision if we fail to see the urgency of knowing and doing God's will. Nothing is more urgent in our lives or in our congregations than yearning to know and do God's will. We must keep our eyes and hearts on our purpose and goal.

God yearns for us to know God's will for the world, for the church, and for ourselves. In fact, the words *yearning* and *will* are interchangeable, though yearning may be less rigid. Think of our yearning to know God's yearning! God's yearning is what God wants for God's people. The faithful response of God's people satisfies God's yearning.

"God wants everyone to know God's will. God doesn't withhold grace, play games, or tease us to test our faithfulness or our

45

worthiness to be trusted with divine insight. God is far more prone to human revelation than I am to divine encounter. God's will is that you and I, everyone, and our faith communities should discern and act upon God's will."[1]

"The promise of spiritual discernment is this: we can know and do God's will. God offers us an up-close and personal relationship. But we can never know God by studying God. We come to know God in the very process of our faithfulness to God— by doing God's will as we know it. The process stops if we are unfaithful to what we have heard, what we have seen, what we know to be God's will."[2]

God's will is not static or fixed in stone. "God does not play games with us as though the divine will were hidden and only God knows what it is. We do not have to sneak up on God or be clever enough to solve the riddle. If we love and walk with God, God and we create the path that leads to our awareness of the divine will as we move along together. Discerning God's will is living fully in the profoundly personal and fulfilling relationship with God that God offers us in Jesus Christ."[3]

Spiritual discernment is not a clever new approach; it is an old approach. It is not an end in itself; it is a lofty means to an end: knowing and doing God's will. If we keep our purpose in sight, we will prevail in the effort of discernment and the church will prosper because the church was created to discern and to implement God's will.

THE URGENCY OF
SPIRITUAL DISCERNMENT

In the beginning, spiritual discernment in an assembly, church board, committee, or prayer group will probably not be an easier, quicker, or smoother way to get the work done. But the church is called to discern God's will for God's people. "Many groups in the church with potential for spiritual discernment do not have business items and long-range decisions to make, e.g., a prayer group. But whether the group has 'work' to do or not, every group in the church is called to utilize spiritual discernment as its way for people to be together; to care for the goals, interests, and concerns of its participants; and to be a vital spiritual factor within the congregation."[4]

Spiritual discernment is the church's way to discover God's will and mission in the world. Will spiritual discernment be a unique practice? Friends (Quakers) believe that it is, and they continue to use it. If a Friend were asked if consensus tends to slow down or derail progress, he or she would probably reply, "That depends on what you consider progress!"

THE CULTURES OF DISCERNMENT

The church over the centuries, and particularly in the twentieth century, has been prone to organize itself and use management methods that have been borrowed from the cultures outside the church. This organizing impulse is vividly described by Richard Reifsnyder in his contribution to *The Organizational Revolution: Presbyterians and American Denominationalism*. Reifsnyder points out that in the twenties, most denominations developed a national church bureaucracy that was patterned after the corporate business world.[5] (We would add that even the "board rooms" which were constructed and appointed in churches were copies of the board rooms of corporate America.) Reifsnyder continues to note how the managerial revolution of the seventies reshaped the church both in denominational structures and in local congregations.[6] He concludes: "The organizational focus of recent years reflects an uncertainty regarding the church's role in a changing society . . . In adapting the values of the culture regarding organizations and process, the church has sought to remedy its own uncertainty about its role.[7]

Do you remember sensitivity training? In the late sixties and early seventies, sensitivity training grew out of the human potential movement. Businesses, schools, and other organizations asked their leaders to participate in small sensitivity groups to help them develop a keen awareness of themselves and the way other people perceived them. In many circumstances, sensitivity training was helpful. However, some people faced emotional turmoil as a result of sensitivity training; as their numbers grew, many who advocated it backed off and the effort fell into disfavor.

Some of the themes and styles of sensitivity training touched into the heritage and practices of religious communities. Many people in the church's small-group movement jumped on the band wagon. Self-understanding was considered to be the vehicle for behavioral change. Throughout history, the church has borrowed from the secular culture. Without doing its theological homework— for example, the experience of grace, unearned love, is a significant basis for behavioral change—the church often bought the assumptions behind sensitivity training and its practices.

Remember MBO—Management by Objective? Setting goals and objectives, determining tactics, and aligning them in proper sequential order for both long-range and short-range planning calendars was a challenge. The church also swallowed MBO. A denominational executive observed, "We worked hard at PBE— Planning, Budgeting, and Evaluating—for twelve years. We were competent professionals, committed to the church, and good at it. But in the end, it did not generate the kind of faith, life, and ministry we longed for." The church is vulnerable. We are apt to turn organizational tools into works; we think that if we are good enough and smart enough and careful enough, we can maneuver our way into a new future. Some theological homework would have suggested to the church that it does not create its own future; it anticipates it as a gift from God.

Without thinking, the church borrows from the culture. It tends to use leadership and management theory for the purpose of organizing and administering the church. Often the church lags behind the culture by ten to twenty-five years. (It uses management theory long since cast aside by schools of management.)

Several recent developments hold promise for the church:

• Management theory increasingly uses religious language— for example, servant, mission, vision, spirit, soul.

• At the same time, the church is hungry for spirituality at all levels of its government and administration (congregation, judicatory, and denomination). A pastor recently observed, "The younger and newer members of my church who are approached to serve on the church board are saying yes only on the condition that the board's work will be framed in a spiritually nurturing process. They are not inclined to serve out of a sense of duty."

• People are dissatisfied with unproductive methods of governance: with the ways church assemblies at all levels meet, interact, and decide.

The combination of the dissatisfaction and spiritual yearning of the church, along with the venture into spirituality by leadership and management theorists, may create an opportunity—a *kairos* moment—for both groups to move creatively into the future. For this to happen, the church will need to let go of its inclination to eagerly copy organizational theories. It will have to return to its own rich traditions and access the practices inherent in the church's ethos to the development of its life and ministry. Then the church can enter into dialogue with the world of management, where a number of church members are already expressing their spirituality in the ways they lead.

Business as usual can no longer be the order of the day for deliberating faith communities. Believing that God has entered into human affairs, religious assemblies will reframe their work as the work of discernment. What is God up to in our world? How can we be a part of God's work? While probing the questions of discernment, the church has a grand opportunity to draw from its traditions and to discern new ways of discerning God's will for a transformed and transforming church.

Prayerful discernment of God's yearning, will, or call is the preferred culture of decision making in the church. Only a process in tune with the church's tradition, ethos, life, and ministry will be appropriate.

However, many cultures of decision making operate in church circles. Some of them are rooted in religious traditions; and others have been imported from education, social science, or business. Depending on the setting and situation, they may or may not be helpful. They are named here in alphabetical order and discussed briefly. These cultures may stand over against, support, or collaborate with the culture of spiritual discernment.

- In an *Autocratic Culture*, decisions rest with one person, who has unchallenged power. He or she may or may not choose to consult with other people or to listen to their advice. No justification is required for any decision he or she makes. The autocrat may assume his or her God-like position, or he or she may be designated by the community.

- In a *Conciliar Culture*, decisions are made by a group of people who have been elected or appointed. They deliberate as an assembly of equals. They may be an elite group, chosen because of their wisdom or position in the community.

- A *Consensus Culture* is characterized by efforts to patiently work through a deliberation to a conclusion that everyone can support. If all are not in total agreement, efforts are made to gain support, permission, or a least assurance that the course of action will not be blocked.

- *Debate Culture* is an ancient classic discipline in which a decision is made after a resolution has been put forth and debated. Arguments both for and against the proposition are presented with supporting data. Credible authorities are cited. The weaknesses of the proposition are attacked and knocked down. Its strengths are defended and propped up. The final judgment is made on the basis of what is left standing.

- In a *Delegation Culture*, an individual or group is charged with the responsibility of making and implementing decisions. Collaboration is desired so that a decision is not made in a vacuum. In a monastic community, for instance, the abbot or abbess consults with the chapter (an assembly of the members of the monastery or their representatives), gleans its wisdom, then makes a decision on behalf of and for the good of the community. The person who has been delegated authority is conscious of the whole community and holds the needs and yearnings of the community in his or her head and heart. In the delegation culture, the community grants and then, in turn, supports the designee's authority.

- In a *Democratic Culture*, decisions are not left in the hands of the elite. Common people are trusted to make decisions on the basis of their own information or information they have been given.
- The *Desire Culture* grew out of ancient spiritual formation practices. In the desire culture, a person's own desires are transformed into desire for the ultimate: God. Self-centeredness, pride, and ambition are redirected or converted to the ultimate object of all desire: to be united with God and God's purposes.
- In an *Emotion Culture*, decisions are based on feelings. Deciding what feels right may lead to shallow and impulsive actions that do not withstand the light of day or the test of time. However, the Jesuits use feelings in a more intentional way. They test a decision by letting it rest near their hearts and by waiting to see if it leads to consolation or to desolation. Does the decision lead them closer to God and result in feelings of peace and well being? Or does it lead away from God and result in feelings of isolation, fear, and distress?
- *Intuition Culture* assumes that different people and groups come to wisdom in different ways. Some need to progress through the steps of deductive reasoning in order to come to a conclusion. Others see in pictures and from inner knowledge. Communities often include people who are gifted with inner sight. The prophets spoke about the pictures they saw. They were either respected by the community because their lives validated their message, or they were decried because they threatened conventional wisdom and the structures of power and privilege. Groups that make decisions do well to listen to people who step over the edges of conventional wisdom. Heretics may be there, but so will prophets. People whose wisdom is intuitive often have difficulty telling what they know within communities organized by efficiency and in which decision making is dominated by assertive, vocal, or rational people.
- In a *Mystical Culture*, decisions are made without respect for intelligence or sense perception. A direct knowledge of God and God's ways, an inner light of God's presence, prompts action. Visions, dreams, and visitations from angels are valid bases for decisions. Respect for mystical paths of knowing vary from one

religious tradition to another. When people with charisma, who are in places of authority or who have the respect of the community, speak of their mystical experience, all debate is usually cut off. The dream is the final word. Joseph Smith's visitation by the angel, Moroni, set the community on a course that was not to be challenged. The community believed that God had spoken.

• *Lottery Culture* involves the biblical practice of casting lots to make choices or to determine outcomes. On the surface, casting lots may seem arbitrary and irresponsible. However, it can be helpful when used responsibly to conclude a decision-making process that has involved careful consideration and prayer. The willingness of the community to cast lots and to support the final decision is critical. By casting lots to select a person or a course of action, the community can break an impasse and get on with its life and work. It can be an expression of faith; God takes our preparatory work and weaves the lottery selection so that God's will and purpose for the good of the community and the world are fulfilled.

• *Mediation Culture* grows out of conflict resolution, which has become a fine art in the church as well as in other organizations. Attempts are made to identify and name the conflict, fathom its depths, explore its underlying assumptions and values, and then to open up channels of communication, foster mutual respect among the conflicting parties, find areas of agreement, and make commitments to work toward resolution of the disagreement. Decisions are based on various levels of agreement.

• *Origin Culture*, which involves tracing an idea, thought, or proposition back to its source, is an ancient practice in the field of spiritual discernment. Did the idea come from the individual? from God? from a good spirit? from an evil spirit? Although some cultures of discerning the spirits may not speak to our contemporary lives, the practice of tracing thoughts and ideas back to their source can be helpful and informative.

• *Parliamentary Culture* is a well-developed process based on a set of rules and procedures that can help a community move through difficult situations and resolve difficult problems. Three principles are essential to parliamentary culture:

1. The rights and unity of the body shall be preserved.

2. The will of the majority shall prevail.

3. The rights of the minority shall be protected.

When properly used, parliamentary law is designed to provide accuracy, efficiency, impartiality, objectivity, and uniformity. For instance, a rule stating that only one matter may be considered at a time creates an orderly process. The limitations of parliamentary culture can be traced to its adversarial nature. The procedures are actually rules for combat. Though they are useful in arbitration and in sorting out different points of view on a designated subject, they also lend themselves to domination by rational, assertive, and verbally oriented participants.

• In a *Political Culture*, decisions are made in the interplay of influence and pressure brought by the groups affected. Compromise, tradeoffs, power, and influence play important roles in a political culture. Politics has a bad name. Too often integrity is compromised and egos prevail, to the detriment of the weak and powerless.

• *Strategic Planning Culture* is an organizational structure. Time frames are determined, goals and objectives are set, and tactics are determined. Success is a high priority, and decisions are made, measured, and evaluated to determine their success.

• *Silence Culture* values solitude. Competing voices are silenced, the clutter comes to rest, and the muddy sediment of activity settles. Seeing clearly, people weigh and consider alternatives that emerge from the silence. The community of Friends (Quakers) has developed a culture of silence in which the sense of the meeting becomes clear.

• In *Wisdom Culture*, the sage plays an important role in the community. Wisdom accrues with age, experience, and observation. The sage sees the results of particular ways of life—for example, he or she sees the ways of the wicked and the ways of the righteous. The elders, who were sages, placed themselves at the gate of the village—the center of commerce and activity—and between the community and the wilderness. The wisdom of the sage was passed down to the young through sayings and stories. The sage embodied wisdom to illustrate and validate his or her message. Church councils often include sages. The group respects their experience and spiritual wisdom and looks to them for guidance in decision making.

• In the *Worshipful-Work Culture*, people gather to make decisions in the context of extended worship. People tell stories and reflect on them in light of the religious tradition. Prayers of thanksgiving and intercession flow from the stories and become part of the agenda. An effort is made to prayerfully discern God's will. Then decisions are lifted up as an offering to God. Paul says, "Present your bodies as a living sacrifice, holy and acceptable to God, which is your spiritual worship" (Romans 12:1). Presenting our bodies means presenting ourselves, our identities, our agenda to God. Worship and work are brought together in ministry.

• In *Visioning Culture*, the role of vision is vital for the community and its leaders. Vision goes beyond strategic planning because it is rooted in God's plan for humanity and for the world. Vision is the big picture, God's kingdom, offered by God as a gift. Once the community has a sweeping view of God's intended future, it can begin to look at particulars through the eyes of spiritual discernment. Discernment and decision making take place in the context of vision and commitment.

The *Culture of Discernment* does not necessarily stand over or against other decision-making cultures. *In fact, it may appropriate many of them into its own process.* In the culture of discernment, church leaders find and order (even through discernment itself) a process of discerning God's will. The process will draw on the faith tradition; adapt helpful aspects of decision making from other religious and secular cultures; and refine the process within the faith, love, and hope of the religious community. We will call insightful and creative leaders of discernment *discernmentarians*.

‑‑ ▦✛▦ ‑‑

We have listed the decision-making cultures in alphabetical order. You may choose to change their order according to their importance for the practice of discernment in your religious community.

(3)

DISCERNMENT: WHO?

ONE AND ONE: INDIVIDUAL SPIRITUAL DIRECTION WITH A PERSON

For the individual, spiritual direction is ordinarily a relationship between two people. We will consider three types of spiritual direction for the individual: historical, formal (spiritual mastery), and popular (spiritual friendship).

Historical Spiritual Direction

Historical direction is the most highly structured and formalized type of spiritual direction. It involves a gifted director, who makes a commitment to enter into a formal, long-term, in-depth relationship with another person, who is admittedly a learner though he or she is usually more mature spiritually than other Christians. We may imagine that only someone who is a serious seeker in the faith would be motivated to enter a relationship with an official director. In the beginning, their relationship is contractual and formal. The directee is accountable to the director.

In the monastic tradition, abbesses and abbots have a classical relationship of spiritual direction with all the other members of the community. Rather than being contractually specified and voluntarily agreed to, guidelines are set forth in, for example, the Rule of Saint Benedict. The relationship between the spiritual director and the novice is usually and preferably lived out in regular, personal, direct, face-to-face sessions. Some instances of spiritual direction have been carried on through correspondence. Records of some long-term relationships are extant and form a remarkable body of content within the Christian tradition, both Catholic and Protestant.

Direction is focused on spiritual mastery and is characterized by:

- advanced spiritual direction;
- a long-term, in-depth relationship between a director and a novice;
- strict accountability to the director;
- the director's decision about when spiritual direction is complete, though the director or the novice may terminate the relationship at any time;
- spiritual regimes specified by director;
- face-to-face sessions or, in unusual circumstances, correspondence;
- spiritual direction between a man and a woman or two people of the same gender;
- confidentiality;
- focus on spiritual growth rather than on problems;
- concern for the novice's awareness and response to the movements of God;
- abbesses or abbots who serve as spiritual directors for individuals and their communities.

Formal Spiritual Direction

Formal spiritual direction is not uncommon today. Like historical direction, it involves an advanced director, contractual agreements, and accountability. Usually the director and the person taking direction agree to a beginning period of sessions. The time frame for sessions is agreed to by both people and may be extended or terminated by either person. The director suggests the shape of contractual agreements and guidelines for accountability, but final agreements are mutually determined and affirmed.

Spiritual direction is not usually centered on a specific problem or crisis; the concern is for naming and responding to the movements of God in a person's life. In the process of direction, a variety of approaches to spiritual discernment may be used: storytelling (talking about life history and experience), reading and studying biblical texts and images, being silent, praying, keeping a journal, participating in spiritual disciplines, guided reading (spiritual biographies and selected novels), and others by mutual agreement.

The desired goal may generally be stated as spiritual mastery. Turning points in the process may occur when the person taking direction feels that he or she has mastered an aspect of his or her life. Then both people may choose to continue the process by working through a new agreement, in which they set new goals and time lines. Or the person seeking spiritual direction may choose to continue with another director.

Someone who has had a good experience in spiritual direction may consider serving in a relationship of spiritual friendship with another person while continuing in a formal relationship of spiritual direction.

In formal spiritual direction, each person senses that the director is farther along on the path of Christian experience and maturity so that he or she serves as a spiritual mentor.

Popular Spiritual Direction
(Peer or Spiritual Friendship)

We refer to spiritual friendship as popular because people enter into the relationship by common consent. Spiritual friends generally have a sense of spiritual simpatico or give-and-take and life experiences that are similar.

Agreements and guidelines for the relationship are mutually explored and affirmed. Time frames are determined. Patterns of relating to each other may be established—for example, spiritual friends may choose to alternate in the role of spiritual director.

Like the participants in a more formal relationship, spiritual friends focus on their experience of the movements of God in their lives. But unlike the two previous models, mutuality is a keynote of the relationship. Each person makes a commitment to walk awhile with the other so that both people may benefit. Spiritual friends generally feel that they are peers in every way.

GROUP AND ONE: GROUP SPIRITUAL DIRECTION WITH A PERSON

Clearness Committee

The Quaker Committee of Clearness works like this: You, the person looking for spiritual direction, "ask three or four special people who are mature and who know and love you to serve as a clearness committee for you. They are not to make decisions for you or even advise you. It is difficult for people you take into your confidence to resist the temptation to tell you what they would do or to tell you what you ought to do. That is why it is so important to have mature friends on a Committee of Clearness."[1] They pray and listen and ask questions. You want them to be attuned to the work of the spirit in their own lives and to be able to see what God is calling forth in your life.

Once you have your Committee of Clearness, you write a brief paragraph or two describing the issue you are facing.

Give it to them when they come together. You may ask, as though you were qualifying a jury, whether any of them have experienced something that would make objectivity difficult or impossible. This is important because it is not their will but God's will you are trying to discern. If anyone feels biased, that person must be excused. Those remaining take your question as a deliberate prayer concern until the next meeting. It is gratifying to know that they are praying with you. There is great power in intercessory prayer and the prayer of the Committee of Clearness is intercessory prayer at its best. At an agreed time, you meet the committee again. Remember, they cannot give advice or advocate a particular solution. They may only ask probing questions for you to consider. Unhurriedly, lovingly, they ask the deep and hard questions without evaluating or criticizing your answers. Through prayer and love for you, under the guidance of the Holy Spirit, they help you consider the discernment issue questions from every side. This meeting will probably be marked with significant periods of silent reflection while your answers are offered and additional questions are framed. When the committee's questions have been answered, all go their way for another period of prayer. Clarity is expected to come! It might come in one meeting or require several. When clearness comes, you thank the group, and the Committee of Clearness is dissolved.[2]

The Committee of Clearness is a classic method of spiritual direction that goes beyond a one-and-one. It involves the group and one or two individuals.

ONE AND GROUP: THE DISCERNMENTARIAN FOR PRIMARY GROUPS

Spiritual Guide

The person who presides at a meeting of Friends (Quakers) is called a clerk. His or her function is quite different from what we normally see in the function of a chairperson. We may choose to call the person who presides at a meeting a chairperson, a facilitator, a moderator, or a discernmentarian.

The designation *parliamentarian* is commonly used to identify leadership in a process of majority rule; in the movements of spiritual discernment, the spiritual guide may be known as a *discernmentarian*. She or he is chosen to guide the deliberations of discernment and eventually to signal the outcome of the meeting. This term may also be applied to a spiritual guide who serves as a back-up resource person for the one presiding at a larger assembly.

In *The Fifth Discipline*, Peter Senge says that a facilitator focuses interactions into dialogue rather than discussion. Whereas discussion is based on assumptions, dialogue calls for suspension of assumptions so that the flow can issue into new meaning and seeing the one thing that needs to be said now.[3]

Therefore, being a spiritual guide for a small or large group is a specialized function. Choosing someone new to serve as discernmentarian at each meeting is probably not wise. The discernmentarian should be someone whom the group trusts and should have enough time and experience in the role to be able to help the group move forward. If the group is new, a discernmentarian should be chosen for the first meeting. Later a permanent choice will be made.

Consideration should be given to the disposition or training needed to be a discernmentarian. The discernmentarian should be spiritually sensitive and caring. He or she should be a good listener and thinker and should have no personal agenda to protect. The discernmentarian should be nurtured in prayer and should be able to identify the spiritual gifts of other people; he or she should be fair. The discernmentarian should have the patience to see an issue through without rushing the process and should be accepted and trusted by everyone in the group.

If the group's regular chairperson has the sensitivity and training of a discernmentarian, she or he may assume both roles. If not, be sure the members of the group know that someone who is properly trained in spiritual discernment will be called forth to guide them in their consideration of particular discernment issues.

In large deliberative bodies, if support is needed by the group's leader, a consultant or resource person may be called the parliamentarian or discernmentarian. The leader who needs assistance in parliamentary rules may be aided by a parliamentarian. The person who presides over a discernment issue may be supported by a discernmentarian.

The Sage

The discernmentarian plays an important role in helping a group through a process of discernment, but other leaders with special gifts will also emerge from the group. One person may have the knack of applying comic relief at just the right time. Another may be the group's historian and story teller. Another may know when to call for silence. Another person will surface as the sage, or wise. one. She or he may not be the most highly educated or the most verbal person in the group. She or he may be young or old, but will possess practical wisdom that the group learns to respect and anticipate.

In Israel's ancient days, sages were called elders. They were shrewd observers of life; they knew what produced happiness, prosperity, justice, peace. They sat at the gates of the village in order to make their wisdom available to the whole community. A body of wisdom literature grew out of their insights. Jesus followed in a wisdom tradition, as did the leaders of the early Christian church.

Groups would do well to call forth, name, embrace, and affirm people who have particular gifts of wisdom so that they will feel free to bring their gifts to the process of discernment. The sage will feel much more confident in bringing forth his or her wisdom if the role has been acknowledged and blessed.

GROUP AND GROUP:
"THE GREAT CLOUD OF WITNESSES"
AND THE COMMUNITY OF FAITH

"The Great Cloud of Witnesses" across the Ages

The person involved in spiritual discernment will do well to hear the voices of the "great cloud of witnesses" (Hebrew 12:1) that surround him or her. They include biblical characters whose lives bear witness to the Spirit and also the saints from across the ages.

The cloud of witnesses in each faith tradition reveals the charism of its founders; the spirituality that made them unique is ingrained in the fabric of the tradition's witness and weaves through its history from year to year, decade to decade, century to century. Discernment occurs in the context of a tradition. We are not imprisoned by our traditions. The voices of tradition can't dictate to us, but they will influence us. We carry on a conversation with tradition, and we should be aware of the voices of our tradition and honor them as part of our reflective process.

Vatican Council II urged religious communities to re-examine in some depth the charism of their founders and the resulting ethos that came to expression in each community. Efforts to reclaim tradition have created new life and vitality for many communities.

The founders of Protestant denominations—Luther, Calvin, Wesley—are relevant to denominations today, especially in times of crisis. The founders of local congregations, who acted on their visions of the church, give new vitality as current leaders rediscover their church's history.

Many Protestants, as well as Roman Catholics, look to the saints of the church, whose spirituality provides inspiration and models of personal discernment.

Hymns are an often-overlooked source of traditional faith. Phrases, lines, or verses of hymns may speak to the process of spiritual discernment or to the situation presented for consideration. In fact, hymns can be sung as part of the process of *relinquishment* or quieting down to listen. Contemporary music and poetry may also be used.

People, living or dead, who have been sources of spiritual wisdom in our own experience should be invited into the process of discernment. After all, they have known us well, and they love us.

The Community of Faith

For the individual, discernment is personal, but never private; it is not done in isolation. Even though the leadings of the spirit may be known only to the individual, the presence of the community and the witness of long-standing Christian traditions will inevitably come into play. We do not engage in the discernment process by accident, or on a whim, or by a quirk of circumstance. We are involved in spiritual discernment because we choose to be and because we are part of a religious community that knows and experiences God.

The person involved in spiritual discernment will be pulled out of isolation by drawing on a trinitarian view of God and on the ways the church has come to know and experience God. We know God as Creator, who called us into being. We know that God is actively working in the world for reconciliation and transformation.

We know God as one who saves us and redeems us, and has called the community into being. The community of faith is a bride, God's beloved. She is a body with many parts who expresses the gifts of God's saving grace.

We know God as the indwelling Spirit who lives in and through the community, bringing power and enlightenment to the people of God. Jesus said that the promised Spirit would lead us into all truth. The Spirit and the Word of God cut to the heart of our deliberations. The Spirit works within the individual and the community to bring to birth decisions and solutions that reveal the will of God. The Spirit grows within to help us uncover the knowledge of God's will that may be buried deep within us.

The process of discernment invites us into the heart and life of the triune God. Decision making can no longer be defined as doing what we think is best; it should be a search for the mind and will of God within a community of people with whom God has chosen to dwell.

Communal discernment is an important discipline. Personal discernment is also vital, but it is always pursued in the context of community. In the community of faith, sisters and brothers pray for one another and for the Holy Spirit's leading. They celebrate their gifts, which are woven into a beautiful tapestry of ministry. In the community, wisdom may be uncovered and clarity may come. (The Quaker practice of providing a Committee of Clearness helps the individual clarify a situation and discern God's will.)

In the community, support and encouragement are readily available, and a person may develop a genuine humility by disclosing his or her thoughts and feelings to a trusted group of people. In the community, people are accountable to one another. There God's gifts and God's activity in the world are discovered and celebrated.

4

DISCERNMENT: HOW?

Having reviewed the church's rich heritage of discernment practices and having looked at the many cultures that contribute to decision making in the church, we can now begin to assemble the movements in the process. We will draw on the authentic discerning graces of our religious traditions in order to provide some practical tools.

Discernment has two sides that are held in relationship with each other; they are the *being* and the *doing* sides. To be discerning is to be steeped in the faith, like saints whose insights were gifts from God. Doing discernment involves the individual and the community in a process that includes specific movements and practices.

The movements of spiritual discernment are not meant to become a mechanical set of procedures, but rather a creative mix that can be adapted by discernmentarians to the situation in which they are involved. The sequence of movements may vary. Some movements in the process may be dropped and others added. The process we suggest is a starting point from which we can continue, probe more deeply, or depart. The process may be used for both personal and communal discernment.

From the threads of the church's long-standing practice of spiritual discernment, the following ten movements will comprise a discernment process that is appropriate for our day. We will name and briefly define them here, then picture them in three visual images. Finally, an in-depth commentary will offer practical insights on ways they can be utilized by individuals and groups.

- *Framing* identifies the focus for discernment of God's will. The matters to be included are arranged into a unified whole. The focus of the exploration is briefly described.

- *Grounding* in a guiding principle jump-starts the process of discernment. The guiding principle is informed by the values, beliefs, and purpose of the discerning community. Boundaries are set.

- *Shedding* lays aside ego, preconceived notions, false assumptions, biases, and predetermined conclusions so that persons involved in discernment can openly consider the matter.

- *Rooting* in the tradition connects religious and biblical stories, themes, and images with the situation at hand. The tradition may confront, confirm, nudge, or even transform the direction of the discernment process.

- *Listening* enables hearing the promptings of the Spirit of God, the voices of all in the discerning community, and the cries of others who may be affected by our discernment.

- *Exploring* frees our playful imaginations to identify possible options and paths that lie within the guiding principle.

- *Improving* works in consultation and prayer to improve each option under consideration until it becomes the best that we can imagine it to be within the yearning of God.

- *Weighing* sorts and tests the options or paths in response to the leading of God's spirit.

- *Closing* brings the explorations to a conclusion, moving toward the selection of an option which is given weight by the Spirit of God and the process in which the community is engaged.

- *Resting* tests the decision by allowing it to rest near the heart to determine whether it brings primarily feelings of consolation (a sense of peace and movement toward God) or desolation (distress and movement away from God).

This presentation in list form will suit the linear thinker, who logically moves from step to step in a process. But for persons who think in pictorial images or in circular fashion, it may seem too confining, perhaps even in contradiction to an open and dynamic process of spiritual discernment. Understanding that persons who engage in discernment have different learning styles and different modes of coming to wisdom, let us offer a range of visual images in addition to a linear listing and description.

Select one or more of the following visual images for your use.

1. Picture discernment taking place in the safety of a small reflection pool.

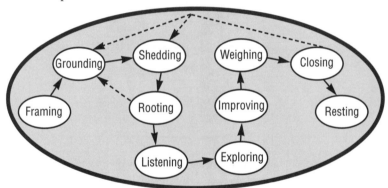

Visual Image #1
Reflection Pool
Stepping Stones for Spiritual Discernment

Ten stepping stones named in the diagram are arranged from one side of the pool to the other. The water in which God's yearning and will are sought provide a safe place. Each stone represents a movement in the process of discernment. Participants may step on each stone in sequence, skip over one, and even come back and revisit one or more stepping stones if they come to impasse.

Also picture discernment taking place as a spiral orbiting around a central core of God's will.

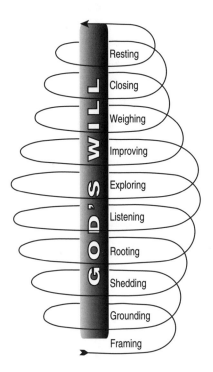

Visual Image #2
Spiral Around Magnetic Core
Movements in Spiritual Discernment

The process begins with framing which is located at the base of this central core, then moves in dynamic fashion round and round until it finally settles and rests on top of the core. The spiral may rotate close to the core or may orbit farther away in open dialogue and exploration. The spiral visually illustrates the opening and eventual closing or settling into a conclusion.

Now picture a grain field, where the seasons of planting, growing, and harvesting provide an image through which one can see the phases of spiritual discernment.

① *Select seeds*   ② *Prepare soil and plant seeds*   ③ *Cultivate plants*   ④ *Harvest yield*

Visual Image #3
Field of Grain
Phases and Steps in Spiritual Direction

Jesus often taught about the nature of the kingdom by pointing to the agrarian practices related to planting, maturing, and harvesting of seed. Four distinct phases can relate to our practice of discernment.

① **A farmer carefully selects the seed.** The right seed needs to be selected to fit the climate and soil conditions. The farmer's "mental model" of a rich harvest frames the final selection from a broad range of possibilities in the same way that the mental model to be framed in discernment relates to seeking God's will.

② **A farmer prepares the soil and plants the seed.** The good soil which is loose, rather than rocky and hard-packed, gives the seed a chance to grow. The seed is grounded in the soil of a guiding principle for our process of discernment.

The seed will die—that is, give itself up for the initial growth of the plant. In like manner, in discernment we are invited to shed, or give up, or come to indifference to anything but God's will.

Even before the new plant sticks its shoot out of the ground, a root system has been put in place. In discernment we *root the process in tradition*—both the ancient biblical tradition and the ongoing traditions and stories of the community of faith.

③ **A farmer patiently cultivates the plants.** The nutrients in the soil, the light and air from the sky, and the moisture from the rains enable the young plant to appropriate these resources, stretch, expand, and come to maturity. The process is a patient one, for neither growth nor the harvest can be hurried.

Discernment is cultivated through *listening*, appropriating all the information and wisdom that is available from God and each other. Explore every possible option to see if God is in it. Work to *improve* each option. The good plants—along with the weak ones and even the weeds—are nourished along side each other and allowed to grow together until harvest. Jesus advised that the wheat and tares should be allowed to grow together. Any intervention would destroy the good plants. At harvest the difference will be obvious.

④ **The farmer harvests the yield.** The good seeds which have been faithfully and patiently tended multiply and produce fruit which makes the hard work and waiting worthwhile.

The winnowing practice of throwing the threshings of wheat into the air for the wind to blow the chaff far away blows the weed seeds some distance, but the good heavy seeds only a short distance. Then harvest *closes* with bagging the separated grain and finally *rests* with the bags safely placed in the storage barn.

In discernment the leadings are *weighed by testing* for the same reason that wheat is harvested so that the good is separated out.

COMMENTARY ON "A GUIDE TO SPIRITUAL DISCERNMENT"

Here we present an in-depth and practical commentary on the ten movements in a process of discernment. As each movement is detailed, it may be located on any one of the three visual images—i.e., stepping stones, the spiral, or the field of grain. The movements can also be tracked in a linear, sequential listing (see pages 92–93).

The discernmentarian who will facilitate these movements with an individual, a small group, or a large assembly, will draw upon these insights as a means of interpreting the dynamics of spiritual discernment and providing a sense of movement for the group. Any movement also triggers resistance, which should be anticipated and taken seriously.

This guide is not meant to be used for discernment fun-and-games. It is not effective with contrived or generic subjects which the participants do not own and cherish. It is a call to prayer. If the spiritual and mystical dimensions are missing, it becomes an empty exercise. It is meant to be used in real-life situations of discernment. The entire discernment experience should have the qualities of prayer, gentleness, harmony, and—at the end of the process—unity.

This guide is offered for use by the discernmentarian with a group. It suggests what she or he may say and do to guide a group through suggested movements of spiritual discernment. The ten movements will be helpful to everyone involved because they provide a quick reference to the process.

SELECTING THE SEED
Framing

In *The Art of Framing*, Fairhurst and Sarr suggest that "mental models" form a foundation for all good framing (p. xiv). "They create a standard, an ideal, or an exemplary case with which to make sense of a situation . . ."[1] The unique "mental model" in our process of framing injects the theological dimension of God's will.

The experience of Trinity Episcopal Cathedral in Sacramento, California, reveals this unique "mental model." James D. Richardson, Senior Warden, writes, "When the Rev. Don Brown came to Trinity Cathedral in 1987 to become its Dean, he brought with him a radical idea for how the Vestry should make decisions. Since Jesus is head of the Church, the Vestry's job is to discern His will. . . . Since the Holy Spirit cannot be of two minds, our job on the Vestry is to discover, as best we can, His will for us stewards of His Church."[2]

Paul D. White, who is assigned to that same parish, observes, "Under this method (Discernment Principle) of parish management, the decision makers must agree to submit to the Lordship of Jesus Christ; to accept Christ as the Head of the Church and, therefore, of the particular parish. . . . All of the participants pray together . . . for Christ to show them what His will is for the parish in any given matter." He goes on to contrast the "American Model," an adversarial method using majority rule, to the "Discernment Model," . . . "where the emphasis is quite different. Instead of a member or group of members being motivated to convince enough voters to accept their point of view, there is an inherent emphasis toward working and praying together to discern the Will of Christ on each issue. . . . There is something profoundly revolutionary about turning to Christ for the decisions affecting His Church. The very act of seriously praying for Christ to reveal His Will to the Church reminds all participants that the Church really does belong to Christ and not to the members of the local congregation."[3]

These testimonies reveal a distinct "mental model" in our framing process which is centered around God's will. This becomes the foundation for the ongoing process which we are now introducing. If you choose the visual image of the stepping stones, framing is the first stone. If you choose the image of the spiral, framing is launched from the base of the magnetic core of God's will. And if you choose the image of the grain field, the frame is created by selecting the seed.

- *Select a subject or an arena for discernment.*

A subject for discernment should be clearly stated and agreed upon by the entire group. If guidance is needed, the question becomes, "God, what are you guiding me/us to do?" If a decision is to be tested, the question is a yes or no question.

In order to determine if a subject or proposition is a realistic discernment issue, framing is essential. Proper framing helps to clarify what we should lay down and what we should pick up on the path to the future we envision. It invites members of the group to agree upon a prayer for discernment.

- *Judge the sense of response.*

Asking the question, "May we consider this as a matter for discernment?" will help the presider test the choice of the group. It should not be called to a vote. Rather, when the matter is presented to the group, the person presiding should judge the sense of response by whatever signs are forthcoming: audible responses for or against considering the matter for discernment, apparent discomfort within the group, or obvious quiet approval.

PLANTING THE SEED
Grounding

- *Ask: What is the guiding principle?*

If you have selected the visual image of the reflection pool, then the second stepping stone you will touch is grounding through the selection of a guiding principle. This stone is positioned in such a manner that you may return to it at any point in the discernment process to reclaim or rename it. If you selected the spiral around a magnetic core, the guiding principle will orbit very close to the core. If you selected the grain field, *grounding* will denote the planting of the seed in the kind of soil that will most likely bear a rich harvest.

Every valid discernment issue should have a stated guiding principle. In the first chapter of Acts, which describes the process used for choosing a replacement for Judas, the guiding principle is clearly stated: *"So one of the men who have accompanied us during all the time that the Lord Jesus went in and out among us, beginning from the baptism of John until the day when he was taken up from us—one of these must become a witness with us to his resurrection"* (Acts 1:21-22). The guiding principle set the boundaries for discernment: Some people were included in the selection process and others were excluded.

Care should be given to forming a guiding principle because

it becomes definitive. In Acts, two candidates—Matthias and Justus—were qualified within the guiding principle. The guiding principle should be specific to the issue and should define both the boundaries of what will be discussed and the aim of the discernment effort.

- *Test one or more suggested guiding principles.*

A guiding principle may be confirmed by scripture or from a previously determined mission or vision statement. There may be a point of struggle in developing a guiding principle. It is usually preferred that the discernmentarian, along with two or three others prepare a tentative guiding principle in order to save time for the larger group. A suggested guiding principle is always subject to refinement or rejection by the body. Even the struggle to designate a guiding principle may be a positive step in the discernment process.

If several guiding principles are offered which are in conflict with each other and no resolution is immediately possible, one alternative is to hold on to them and continue through the next two discernment movements. Then return to grounding in an attempt to find resolution. If there is still no agreement, continue on to see if it will work out in the process as trust is built in the group. You may return at any time to reconsider. If your image is the reflection pool, come back and re-step on this stone.

If there is controversy about which principle should guide discernment and the group cannot agree on a final choice, the discernmentarian may suggest a more generic guiding principle, such as "God's will: nothing more; nothing less; nothing else." A generic guiding principle may suffice as a compromise if it sets desirable and definite boundaries and suggests an end result and a grounding that everyone can affirm.

Shedding

Shedding means naming and laying aside anything that will deter the person or group from focusing on God's will as the ultimate value.

What needs to die in me/us in order for God's gifts and direction to find room in our lives?

Again, listen to James D. Richardson. "This means we are not on the Vestry to pursue our private agenda. We are not on the Vestry to legislate for our pet causes or to settle scores. Discernment provides a different focus to our deliberations as a vestry. When we forget that focus we fall apart as a group. . . . Sometimes we find it very hard to leave our personal agendas at home. . . . The process requires each of us to look inside ourselves and ask questions about why we are advocating a certain position or objecting to something that rubs us the wrong way. Are my prejudices at play? Are my feelings well founded? What would Jesus do? Am I listening? We do not have the luxury of protest votes."[4]

Peter Senge speaks of the need to "suspend assumptions" in order for genuine dialogue to take place. That does not mean getting rid of them, but naming them for all to see.[5] Even naming them offers a degree of release.

In the image of the pool, the shedding stepping stone may be slippery, so take time to settle onto it. With the spiral image, it circles close to the mystery of God's presence because our ego drive becomes sublimated to that of Christ. The image of the grain field reminds us that the seed must undergo a type of death when it is placed in the ground.

- *Guide the process of indifference.*

The word indifference is usually thought to be a negative word. To say "I am indifferent" means "I am not interested" or "I don't care" or "count me out."

As a principle of discernment, indifference is a positive word, deep in meaning and rich in the Christian tradition. To say "I am indifferent" does not mean "I don't care," but rather, "I don't value anything as much as I value knowing and doing God's will." It means that I am indifferent to matters of ego, prestige, politics, personal ownership, pride, favor, comfort, advantage, and so on. **I am indifferent to everything but God's will.** The questions a person answers in the process of indifference are these: What am I willing to let die to give God room to start something new? What will I lay aside or leave behind so that I will be open to new gifts of grace or new expressions of ministry?

If indifference is a coveted place to be, it is not easy to attain. People involved in the process of shedding may humble themselves or give up values they usually cherish in pursuit of the greater good. The process may mean spiritual death and resurrection.

Someone may sense an immediate state of indifference on a particular matter and will be able to announce his or her indifference easily and quickly; another person may struggle with indifference.

The process of coming to indifference includes the steps or changes that are needed for each person to become indifferent to everything but God's will. Each person in the group will determine his or her own process of indifference. The process may be introspective or it may be expressed verbally. Whichever, the process of indifference is not optional for people who want to be serious about discerning God's will.

A group may also have an undeclared process that they move through to indifference. The group's process may only be obvious after the fact and may include talking, listening, praying, dying and rising again to new levels of vision and passion.

Whereas the individual may feel that becoming indifferent is private, members of the group may encourage and guide one another through the process by openly talking about the issue of giving up personal agendas and coming to indifference for the greater good of knowing the divine will. The process may form the group as a community. Perhaps, as Bonhoeffer suggests, the community of Christ can only be formed when individual "wish dreams"—even hopes and dreams for the community—have been shattered.

The discernmentarian should have a solid grasp of the rich concept of indifference and should devote time and effort to helping the participants to fully comprehend it, even though the process may be somewhat difficult.

- *Test for indifference:*
  Ask: *"How many are indifferent to all but God's will?"*

The *process* of indifference usually involves several loosely defined steps. They may be formalized, or individuals may engage in the process intuitively.

The *test* for indifference will be the final step, when the discernmentarian asks, "How many are indifferent to all but God's will?"

The question should not be voted on. It is a question that each person should consider in his or her own mind and heart. One person may answer with affirmation; another may talk about the influences that are obstacles to indifference. She or he may say, for example, "I want to be indifferent, but I have a lot of sweat equity invested," or "My ego is a factor here," or "I am having trouble letting it go." He or she trusts the group enough to express his or her confusion or difficulties, rather than keeping feelings a secret.

Responses such as these should not prompt ridicule, censure, or chastisement, but should be valued as honest statements of a deeply concerned and struggling person. When expressed, the group can proceed, but should be sensitive to the person's struggle.

It is best if everyone affirms his or her indifference; but if that cannot be done, it is better for the group to know the heart of each person. Knowing where everyone stands in the process of indifference will help the group to work through the process of corporate discernment.

Allowance needs to be made for persons to respond at various levels of indifference. Various levels may be conditioned by the degree of trust that each participant senses in the group. As a general rule, allow the trust indicator which lies within each person to determine the degree to which self-disclosure of deeply held assumptions and feelings will be expressed. As the discernment group continues to build trust with each other in the process, the shedding may continue in a growing fashion. A second factor relates to the depth of the issue which is under consideration. Invite shedding only in proportion to the issue. And a third factor could relate to the operating norms of the particular group—holding the cards close to the chest or laying them on the table. The fact that this group's identity has been formed in faith roots—where the ultimate model can be seen in the Christ who shed his all and prayed "not my will, but yours be done" (Luke 22:42), invites a much deeper level of relinquishment than may be called for in most human associations.

The group's awareness of each person's state of indifference should not be determined by a vote, but by honest conversation and genuine listening.

When the discernmentarian senses that everyone has been heard, he or she should make a summary statement, such as, "I sense that we are indifferent on this matter," or she or he may need to say to one or more persons who could not come to indifference: "We thank you for your honesty."

Indifference is, at the same time, a process of discernment, a test of reality, and a gift of grace.

Shedding is not only an individual process. Groups face the same invitation to become indifferent to all but God's will. Using the pronoun *we* will help members of the group come together and confront the challenge of indifference together.

- *Use the pronoun "we."*

There will be times when the discernmentarian can invite the members of the group to move from understanding themselves as individuals to sensing that they are united on indifference as a community, from *I* to *we*. This is possible only when each person acknowledges his or her indifference. It may be symbolized, in a small group, by inviting the participants to join hands and to say a brief prayer of thanksgiving for shared indifference. (If everyone has not expressed indifference, omit the symbol of unity. The discernmentarian should not try to move from I to we if one or more people have not expressed indifference.)

The questions of indifference are these: Are we willing to let something die to give God room to start something new? What will we lay aside or leave behind so that we will be open to new gifts of grace or new expressions of ministry?

Rooting

In spite of the suggestions of some, we have chosen to hold to the rooting movement at this point in the discernment process. They say we should always begin discernment by rooting in tradition. But in this entire process, a new foundation has been laid upon which framing and grounding can now be tested and deepened. In fact, you may choose to return to those steps for reframing and adjusting or resolving the guiding principle, after you have rooted in both the biblical and historic traditions. Restep on those stones; take the appropriate orbit around the magnetic core of God's will; or reselect the seed and soil plot if that is needed.

- *Ask: "What biblical images or texts come to mind?"*

Invite the group to suggest Scripture that relates to the issue for discernment. Biblical images or texts make their own contribution to the discernment process. Also, ask the participants to suggest images, themes, stories, or people in Scripture that make connections with the issue they are considering. This is subjective, and the connections may be seen clearly by only one person in the group. However, participants should not have to defend their suggestions or justify their choices. The Scripture passages may or may not be discussed.

Beyond biblical references, the Christian tradition and the history of the local congregation may provide the group with ways to view the topic. Gifts from the arts and great hymns of the church may also be mentioned. Recalling stories from other sources help the group form a corporate memory.

After the participants have had time to speak, the discernmentarian may move directly into silent prayer.

CULTIVATING THE PLANTS
Listening

Peter Senge adds that in addition to suspending assumptions for dialogue, the participants should see each other as colleagues.[6]

Let us continue Trinity Cathedral's story. "For this process to work, we must have tremendous respect for each other, and that means we must listen well to each other. Each member of the Vestry counts; no one is more important than another (Richardson). "The underlying concept is that Christ speaks to His Church in a variety of ways and through a variety of people; sometimes, even just one person. . . . The discernment model invites the influential and the non-influential to speak to what they discern is Christ's will without risking rejection by the other decision makers. On the other hand, the American model presents a substantial risk of rejection and often results in many people refusing to voice their feeling for fear of rejection. A crucial aspect of the discernment model is that all members respect the views of each member, indeed, that all members invite the views of each member."[7]

In the pool image, you now take a far-reaching step to the next stone. In the spiral image, the orbit swings wide to gather much information. And in the grain field, the new plant shoots up and stretches its branches to the winds and toward the light.

- *Ask: "Whose voices do we need to hear?"*
  Say: "Let us pray in silence, seeking to discern God's will."
  (Specify the length of time allowed for prayer.)

Listening is essential in discernment. Listening to one another, to the cries of people in need, and to the Spirit of God are all necessary. Listening may include gathering information and conducting interviews with people outside the group, especially if a response to their yearnings is the focus of discernment. Include listening to the voices on the edge as well as those in the center.

The discernmentarian may introduce a period of silent prayer so that the group can listen to the inner prompting of God's Spirit.

The group moves from the "house" (the small group) to the "closet" (solitude). Prayer should be focused on the discernment issue. The time devoted to silence should be announced, and the discernmentarian should watch the clock. As an alternative, the participants may scatter to spend time alone and agree to reconvene at a specified time.

If the discernmentarian judges that participants have had limited experience with silence, five minutes may be sufficient; or the leader may announce a longer period and provide suggestions on ways to enter creatively into silence.

Invite the participants to pray and to listen. Sitting in silence after they have prayed may allow them to be more open to the Holy Spirit and to be present to the Spirit in deeper ways that only silence will permit.

Listening and the feelings that result may be valuable responses to the movement of the Holy Spirit. As they pray and listen, encourage the group members to be aware of their deep, inner feelings. Are they feeling joy, peace, a sense of right, a movement toward God? These may be feelings of consolation.

Encourage the participants to be aware of distress. Are they ill-at-ease, troubled, or concerned? Do they feel confused? These may be realistic movements reflecting the absence of the Holy Spirit. Following prayer, participants may initially feel both consolation and desolation—but if they continue to pray and to listen, eventually (though perhaps not in five or ten minutes), one or the other will predominate. Encourage the group to be sensitive to their feelings of consolation or desolation throughout their silence and to continue to pray and to listen, at later times, until they sense that discernment has come.

After the period of silence, invite the group members to talk about their experience. Assure them that they do not necessarily have to have clear feelings of consolation or desolation as an immediate validation of the presence of the Spirit. Suggest that they continue in prayer and silence at a later time and for as long as it takes to discern God's will.

Exploring

The grain field provides a safe place for the new plant to grow and develop. On the image of the reflection pond, a cluster of stepping stones—near and far (an easy step or a far reach)—may be touched. In the image of the spiraling orbits around a magnetic core, the circling may continue round and round until a few distinct orbiting paths have been established. Each shoot from the ground may now support several branches. In like manner, in discernment we explore various options or paths that could be followed.

- *Ask: "What are possible options or paths within the guiding principle?"* (List on a large sheet of paper possible options suggested by the group.)

In discernment, nothing is to be hidden or ignored. All suggestions may shed light on the subject. The group should feel free to identify as many options or alternative paths as they can. Each option will be welcomed. For example, if the issue is painting the building red, possible options may be not painting the building, painting it another color, tearing down the building, putting on siding, moving the building, selling the building. The more legitimate options to be considered, the better for discernment.

The discernmentarian may begin by stating any obvious options and/or by inviting the group to suggest options. The participants should be in a free-wheeling and exploratory mode while suggesting options. Then the list may be reduced to a manageable number—three—of the best of all suggested options.

The goal is to identify all possible directions or alternatives. Each option (or the two or three top selections) may be finally put before the group. In the Quaker tradition a clerk states the option as a "minute" which is somewhat like a motion in majority rule. Each option is offered like a trial balloon to determine if it needs to be restated for more clarity.

Improving

The new branches which have been produced on the plant in the grain field now need the opportunity to develop to maturity. They will draw moisture, light, and nutrients which will enable them to offer a full, ripe ear or pod of seeds. Within the visual image of the spiral, the circling continues at this level so that each orbit adds good to good, thereby enhancing each particular option. And the image of the reflection pond places us on the step of "bettering it up."

- *Say: "Now improve each option. Make each option the best it can be."*

Improving is a marvelous concept that is particular to discernment and sets it apart from parliamentary procedure or majority rule. In the process of majority rule, the goal is to find the lowest common denominator, the proposition on which most of the people can agree. In discernment, the goal is to make each option the best it can be.

Invite the group to improve each option. Keep notes so that when the process is complete, the issue will be fully pinpointed. Your notes should include the best possible picture of the issue on as many options as the group has considered.

Take time to improve the options. The participants may choose to work together or to spend time in silence before reporting to the group. Through discernment, God's will is more likely to be found in the most rather than in the least.

The discernmentarian attempts to pull together what has been improved prior to weighing each option and closing. The minute for each option is now restated by the discernmentarian or by the group.

To finalize this matter, the discernmentarian:

a) is interested in where the group is at this point in the process.

b) listens for directions which the process takes, for points of clarity, or conclusions and leadings, and offers them to the group for response.

c) refines a statement that discussion may reshape.

d) Asks: "Is anyone uncomfortable with proceeding in the way just stated?"

HARVESTING THE YIELD
Weighing

Weighing allows the discerning person or group to move toward a preference for the paths or options which have been identified and improved. It is a way of moving toward closure and bringing the process to a conclusion—drawing upon various ways of coming to wisdom and following God's guidance.

- *Ask: "Upon which option or path will the Spirit rest?"*

- *Ask: "How can we come to a preference for a particular path?"* (Introduce several ways to put each option to a testing of spirits.)

Before closing the discernment dialogue, the paths or options which have been identified and improved now can be tested and weighed. In this process, more than human judgment is involved. While using all of the means of coming to wisdom—the symbolic, intuitive, rational, etc.—the discerner stands on holy ground, trusting the working of the indwelling Spirit to be actively engaged in the process. Both traditional spirituality and contemporary faith practices can be drawn upon.

Select one of the following means of weighing:

• From the Jesuit practice of rigorous and vigorous mental examination, draw a line down the middle of a page and list the pros and cons for each option.

• From the biblical witness, "by their fruits you shall know them," list the likely fruits which each path would produce.

• From the church father, Origen, trace the source of the thoughts. Are any from God's Spirit? Are any rooted in the devil's work of making sin attractive? Do any arise from the drive of human ego?

- From John Cassian, apply the five-way test of the money changer to each option.
    1) Is it filled with what is good for all?
    2) Is it heavy with the fear of God?
    3) Is it genuine in the feelings that underlie it?
    4) Is it lightweight because of human show or because of some thrust toward novelty?
    5) Has the burden of vainglory lessened its merit or diminished its luster?

- From the Jesuits, place each path near the heart.
    1) Is there consolation—a sense of peace and movement toward God?
    2) Is there desolation—a sense of dis-ease and movement away from God?

- From the practices of silence and solitude, allow the Spirit to "lure" you to a particular path where the Spirit rests.

- From biblical launched imagination, read John 14:1-3. Jesus offers to go ahead and prepare a "place" for us in God's "house." Imagine entering a large mansion-type house. Jesus meets and greets you at the door. How does he greet you? What does he say? He escorts you step by step up a long spiral stairway. At the top, you sit together on a bench in a large, round, open hallway that is flooded with natural light from a skylight. Around the hallway are several doors—in fact, the same number of doors as options you are considering in your discernment. When you are ready, Jesus offers to accompany you to each door, then gently opens them one at a time, allowing you to peer into each room. What do you see in each?

- From the art of guided imagery, begin by selecting a symbol—something you could draw or fashion—for each option. Then, in your imagination, take a trip to a chapel or to a beautiful secluded meadow with a reflection pond. Upon arrival, allow colorful appointments to embellish your holy place. Invite a holy and wise person to enter the space and greet this Sage. Receive the Sage's greeting in return. Then, as you sit together, imagine each symbol which you have selected entering the space, interacting with the environment and with each other until they come to rest. Note where and how they rest and in what relationships. Then say good-bye to each symbol. Receive the Sage's parting words and gestures, and return to the location of your discernment.

The discernmentarian should be open to the possibility that more time is needed or desired. If so, he or she should test for clarity and direct the group accordingly. Or the discernmentarian's sense may be that the group is ready to proceed.

The decision should not be subject to a vote at this time. The discernmentarian should first try to sense the response of the group and offer a choice.

a) Say: "I sense that we are ready to respond."

b) Or say: "I sense that you wish to pray and consider this matter further," and suggest a time for further consideration.

If the discernmentarian judges that the group is not ready to respond or is in any way challenged by the group, she or he may suggest that more time is needed.

The discernmentarian should be definite in offering an alternative time for further consideration: respond later in the meeting, at the end of meeting, at the next meeting, or at a called meeting. The time should be negotiated by the body and strictly honored.

Closing

After drawing a distinction between discussion ("decisions are made . . . which converge on a conclusion or course of action") and dialogue ("different views are presented as a means toward discovering a new view"), Peter Senge observes that "a learning team masters movement back and forth between dialogue and discussion."[8]

The prior three movements (listening, exploring, and improving) fall into the dialogue category—where there is a constant opening up for new insight and wisdom. Now, in the image of the grain harvest, the process moves to the discussion category—to conclusion, or closing down on a decision or new direction. The rhythms of planting and reaping provide good illustrations of this movement. We cannot keep matters up in the air forever. We live within spiritual attention spans and time boundaries. In the reflection pool image, we are nearing the other side. In the spiral image, we are slowing down and orbiting closer to the magnetic core.

The following steps may now be taken to bring final closure.

1) Test for consensus.

The discernmentarian, acting in the tradition of the Quaker clerk, may offer a final minute—one that seems to be most weighty—for a test for consensus. Ask participants to choose one of the following levels of response to the minute:

a) "I like the minute as stated." (Consensus)

The final statement of the minute (proposition) is acceptable to the person. If everyone responds positively, the group has come to a consensus.

b) "I am concerned, but will support the minute." (Consensus)

The person basically affirms the statement. She or he might say, "If I were making the decision alone, I would say it differently; but I feel that we have discussed it thoroughly and that everyone has been heard. It is not exactly the statement I would like, but it is close enough. I will not block it." If such a position is stated, it should give the group a healthy warning to be careful and thoughtful for any of the reasons the individual has mentioned. It is at least a request to not rush to judgment without due consideration. If the group members either support the statement totally or support it with some reservations, the group has come to consensus.

c) "I am uneasy for these reasons, but will stand aside." (Consensus)

d) "I cannot support the minute." (Non-Consensus)

This is a stop sign! It indicates that the body has not reached full consensus on the proposal.

The group may choose to stop the process or give the subject more consideration. If efforts to reach consensus fail and the person cannot in good conscience change his or her response, the discernmentarian may ask the person if he or she feels able to stand aside, so as not to block the rest of the group. The person's reasons for not supporting the minute would be recorded.

• If the group is seriously divided, not yet ready to conclude, or at an impasse, select one of the seven options listed below. (Seriously divided means no consensus, contrary feelings, and an argumentative attitude about the outcome. Not yet ready to conclude means that more time is needed for prayer, information gathering, or discussion; the body will not rush to judgment. At an impasse means that the members of the group are obviously too far apart to anticipate consensus.)

1) *Reconsider the guiding principle, test again for indifference, and repeat the rest of the discernment process.*

If discussion has shed new light on the proposal, invite the group to either reaffirm the guiding principle or to reshape it. Then test again for indifference so that the group will know how each person feels about the proposal as it relates to his or her discernment of God's will. Then repeat other steps in the process as needed to come to consensus.

2) *Take time for further prayer and reflection.*

Prayer and reflection may shed more light on the proposal than further discussion will. The group may choose to spend a week or a month in prayer and further reflection. Even if the group holds expediency as a value, and discerning God's will as its highest value, time may be an aid to discernment rather than an obstacle, because time for prayer often brings light.

3) *Cast lots.*

In Acts 1:26, the disciples cast lots to determine the person who would replace Judas. Both Matthias and Justus were qualified according to the disciples' guiding principle, so the disciples were choosing between equally acceptable options.

When a situation offers several good choices and the group doesn't want to vote down a good option and make it a loser, the participants may decide to cast lots. The option which is drawn by lot will be chosen. Before action is taken, the members of the group should agree to make a final decision by casting lots and should also agree to support the outcome.

4) *Appoint one person to decide for the group.*

In a few situations, members of the group may select one person whom the group trusts to make the final decision. Before action is taken, the group should pray for this person and agree to follow the option.

5) *Vote by majority rule* (simple majority, 2/3, 3/4, or 4/5).

Voting is an option, especially in a large deliberative body. The sting of voting, which creates winners and losers, will be removed if everyone has been included in the discernment process and each person feels that he or she has been heard. The body may properly decide that voting is both fair and expeditious in the situation.

6) *Count only the "yes" votes.*

This option is helpful when a specific number of people are needed for starting a project or ministry (see page 135).

7) *Drop it.*

If the body or group discerns no leading in the matter, celebrate the discernment, drop it, and move on.

Resting

The final stepping stone on our visual image of the reflection pool can now be touched. How does it feel? The spiraling bit of energy has come to rest on the magnetic core of God's will. Is this a comfortable place to be? The grain has been bagged and is now safely in the storage barn. Are you worried about bugs? or fire? or storm? or thieves?

Resting becomes the final movement in our process of spiritual and prayerful discernment.

• *Invite the participants to rest the decision near their hearts as they look for consolation or desolation.*

• *Ask, "Is our decision God's will: nothing more, nothing less, nothing else?"*

In discernment, resist the temptation to rush forward even when a matter seems properly concluded. If time permits, invite the group to rest in the final conclusion. How does the decision sound in the parking lot after the meeting? How does it feel after sleeping on it overnight? How does it sit when explaining it to a friend? a foe? How do people who did not participate in the process respond to it?

Encourage the group members to put the matter to the test of the heart to see if it brings consolation or desolation. Does the decision bring peace and draw the group closer to God and each other or does it result in distress and move the group away from God?

The following is a simple statement of the highest value in the process of spiritual discernment. **God's will: nothing more, nothing less, nothing else**. Invite the group to consider their decision in light of the purpose and goal of spiritual discernment: Is this the will of God, yes or no?

—•— ◄► —•—

When you have finished the exercise in discernment, review the experience and make notes on how it went, what you learned about the dynamics and principles of discernment and consensus, and what you discovered about God's will.

In prayer and patience, repeat the process with other agenda items. Remember that you have experience in an adversarial or majority rule culture of decision making. Give yourself helpful experience and adequate time to begin to seriously practice spiritual discernment, a new way of doing ministry and being the church.

A GUIDE TO DOING
PRAYERFUL DISCERNMENT

D
I
S
C
E
R
N
M
E
N
T
A
R
I
A
N

① SELECTING THE SEED
Framing
Select a subject or an arena for discernment.
▶ *May we consider this as a matter of discernment, asking,*
   "God, is this your will, yes or no?" *
(Judge the sense of response.)

② PREPARING THE SOIL
Grounding
▶ *What is the guiding principle?*
(Test one or more suggested guiding principles.)

Shedding
Process of indifference.
Test for indifference:
▶ *How many are indifferent to all but God's will?*
(Acknowledge all who are not indifferent.)
▶ *We thank you for your honesty.*
▶ *"I" and "we"*

Rooting
▶ *What are the biblical images or texts that come to mind?*

③ CULTIVATING THE PLANTS
Listening
▶ *What voices do we need to hear?*
▶ *Let us pray in silence for _____ minutes, seeking to*
   discern God's will.

Exploring
▶ *What are the possible options or paths within the guiding*
   principle?
(List before the group.)

Improving
▶ *Now "better up" (or improve upon) each option. Make each*
   the best it can be.

---

*Triangles (▶) denote text to be spoken aloud by the discernmentarian.

D
I
S
C
E
R
N
M
E
N
T
A
R
I
A
N

④ **HARVESTING THE YIELD**

Weighing (the options)

1. Rigorous, vigorous mental examination
2. List the fruits
3. What is the source?
4. Cassian's five-way test
5. Consolation or desolation
6. Does the Spirit *lure* you?
7. Using biblical imagination
8. Using guided imagery
▶ *Are we ready to close? Does this matter need more prayer and reflection, or are we ready to respond?*

(Judge the sense of response.)

Closing

Select a minute.

▶ *May we proceed in the way just stated?*

Levels of response to the minute (each chooses one of the four):

1. I like the minute as it is stated. *(Consensus)*
2. I am concerned, but will support the minute. *(Consensus)*
3. I am uneasy . . . reasons . . . but will stand aside. *(Consensus)*
4. I cannot support the minute. *(Non-Consensus)*

If seriously divided, not there yet, or at an impasse:

1. Revisit the guiding principle and test for indifference, then repeat the discernment movements above.
2. Take time for further prayer and reflection.
3. Cast lots.
4. Appoint someone to decide for the group.
5. Vote by majority rule.
6. Count only the "yes" votes.
7. Drop it.

Resting

Test of the heart.
Consolation? Desolation?

GOD'S WILL: NOTHING MORE . . .
NOTHING LESS . . .
NOTHING ELSE . . .

5

DISCERNMENT: WHERE?

BIBLICAL METAPHORS FOR DISCERNMENT: SANCTUARY, HOUSE, CLOSET

Now let us consider the three arenas in which the practice of discernment takes place. Discernment finds its place in the minds and hearts of the individuals who prayerfully seek to fulfill God's yearnings. Discernment also takes place in small groups of people: a study group, a prayer group, a ministry group, a committee, a church board or council, the staff of a church or religious association. Discernment is a way for a large assembly to make policies and to plan its life and ministry, so discernment also finds a place in open meetings of the congregation or in regional or national gatherings of a religious denomination.

Historically, discernment has been an individual pursuit. Today, we seek to explore the possibilities of using communal discernment in both small and large groups.

To begin, we look for clues in Scripture. There we find three metaphors describing the places of prayer and worship; the images in Scripture speak directly to the practice of discernment. The biblical metaphors, in Acts 2 and Matthew 6, provide a framework for our consideration of personal and corporate discernment. The places of prayer interact with one another to create the rhythm or dynamic for discernment. The three metaphors are the sanctuary, the house, and the closet.

Sanctuary, house, and closet are referred to in Acts 2:46-47: "Day by day, as they spent much time together in the temple [sanctuary], they broke bread at home [house] and ate their food with glad and generous hearts [closet], praising God and having the good will of all the people." A more direct reference to the closet as a place of prayer is in Matthew 6:6, "Whenever you pray, go into your room and shut the door and pray to your Father who is in secret; and your Father who sees in secret will reward you."

Jesus practiced prayer and discernment in solitude, in the privacy of his own mind and heart. He went to the desert, or place of safety, to fast and to pray, to be tempted and to discern the spirits. He left the crowds and his closest friends to pray alone. He taught his disciples to go beyond a public display of prayer to talk intimately with God, as a child would talk with a loving parent.

Jesus practiced prayer and discernment in the intimate community of the twelve. He led the disciples to reflect theologically on their daily experiences and connected them to the tradition of Abraham, Sara, Moses, Miriam, and the prophets.

In the intimate group, there were no hiding places. There, the disciples struggled with their egos and vied for places of honor and power. They faced and named their callings, their denials, their love, and their fears, as they sought to be faithful to God's yearnings for them and for the world God loved.

Jesus practiced prayer and discernment in large crowds and in the sanctuary. "Jesus went throughout Galilee, teaching in their synagogues and proclaiming the good news of the kingdom and curing every disease and sickness among the people. So his fame spread throughout all Syria. And great crowds followed him from Galilee, the Decapolis, Jerusalem, Judea, and from beyond the Jordan" (Matthew 4:23-25). Jesus taught in the synagogues and in the Temple, where he insisted, "My house shall be called a house of prayer for all the nations" (Mark 11:17).

Each of the three settings offers a unique way of practicing discernment. The closet, or solitude, is a place that is free of distractions. There, an individual may lay aside everything that steals his or her energy and may focus on the presence and will of God. The closet offers a quiet space to listen for the voice of God.

The house offers the experience of a small community in which people know one another's names and stories; they know what each person brings to the process of discernment, his or her gifts, struggles, and journeys. A community of trust is built, not on human efforts or intelligence, but through God's grace, reconciliation, and forgiveness. In a house, people trust one another and can risk the honesty that discernment needs. A household tends to be personal, informal, playful, and interactive. People are creative because they can bounce ideas off one another's imagination and wisdom.

The sanctuary offers public recital of the drama of grace. In the sanctuary, the great resources of tradition have been gathered over the ages and form a witness wider than an individual, group, church, or generation. The sanctuary invites participants into the traditional drama. Connections are made. Mystery is acknowledged. The readings, stories, liturgies, hymns, artistic environment, preaching, fellowship, and prayers are corporate. They form and inform discernment of God's will, offering specific guidance and bursts of insight.

While the sanctuary, house, and closet offer three distinct settings for discernment, they are interdependent. If we confine prayer to only one of the three, we will experience a void, an impoverishment in our spiritual lives.

All three of these metaphors should properly be included in our ecclesiology, our understanding of the church. They are rich images that define the rhythm of discernment and propel us forward on the quest for God's will. They are three settings; but more than settings, they are like music, the movements of a symphony. To use one of the metaphors without the others is to bog down the process of discernment and to rob it of the joy of intended discovery of God's will.

The essential rhythms of governance within large deliberative bodies may be found in these three metaphors. The sanctuary—or assembly—comprises the whole community of faith or a large group of delegates who gather for the purpose of discernment. The house—or small group—either stands on its own (a prayer group) or practices discernment as part of an assembly (a committee of a conference). The closet—or solitude—refers to the process of discernment in the heart and soul of the individual, where God alone is Lord of the conscience.

As we explore the possibilities for discernment in the three different settings, we will use the words *assembly*, *group*, and *individual* to refer to the sanctuary, house, and closet, knowing that they carry with them the rich traditions of the biblical images.

MAPPING OR GRAPHING A PROCESS FOR DISCERNMENT

Even though discernment, at its core, is a way of life, a way of praying, a way of relating and responding to God, there are structures and processes that guide our quest. If no spiritual guidance is available, assemblies, groups, and individuals may wander in a wilderness of confusion and disarray; but the Spirit of God offers gifts that order the faith community in its reflection and decision making. Time-honored practices from traditions of faith are available and can be brought to bear on the process of discernment. Instead of relying solely on the practices of secular decision-making cultures, we call on discernmentarians to help root discernment in the soil of the church's tradition.

The discernmentarian will work prayerfully, creatively, and collaboratively with assembly representatives, small groups, and individuals to create a tentative map or graph to follow during the process.

When we plan a trip, we get out a map, spread it out on a table, and locate our destination. Then we plot a course to our destination, with stops along the way that will enrich our trip or provide nourishment and rest. We pace the trip, giving consideration to our resources and time. Once we have located the places where we will stop, we draw a line connecting our starting point with each stop and finally on to our destination.

For our purposes in mapping discernment movements, both a map and a chart will be used. The Discern-O-Map will be used by the discernmentarian to plot the future course of our process. Connecting lines can be drawn from points that have been plotted on the grid of our ten movements and three settings (individual, group, and assembly). Hereafter we refer to it as "the map." Here is a picture of a blank Discern-O-Map.

Discern-O-Map

Place a dot at the level where each movement will take place. Then connect the dots with solid lines for formal contact and dotted lines for informal attention.

Setting	Frame	Ground	Shed	Root	Listen	Explore	Improve	Weigh	Close	Rest
Assembly										
Group										
Individual										

Anticipated dates and times may be inserted to keep the process on track. Discernment is rightfully a patient process, and a group that rushes to judgment is apt to meet with pitfalls and obstacles. Time for discernment should be free of the threat of calendar or clock. Still Easter or Christmas arrive on time, and Advent and Lent will not wait for a committee's work. Because of hotel reservations and transportation commitments, even large national assemblies need to begin and end on given dates. Recording tentative dates on a map for discernment is helpful, as long as the group feels free to depart from them and to give the Spirit the time needed to conclude the process.

The Discern-O-Chart will be used by those who are in the midst of a discernment to record experiences and impressions. The grid offers spaces for journal notes. Hereafter we will refer to it as "the chart." Here is a picture of a blank Discern-O-Chart.

Discern-O-Chart

Please record, in the appropriate columns, events, contacts, prayers, wisdom, and leadings of the Spirit.

Setting	Frame	Ground	Shed	Root	Listen	Explore	Improve	Weigh	Close	Rest
Assembly										
Group										
Individual										

The chart may serve as a recording device to keep track of where an individual or group has been in the discernment process. Sometimes, individuals who are involved in spiritual discernment feel as if they are stuck or going in circles. The chart offers a way for them to assess progress. It helps discerners see where they are in relation to the ten movements. It presents a historical record of each phase, culminating in closing and resting, when the will of God is discerned and decisions have been made.

On the map, the route may begin at any one of three locations: the sanctuary (assembly); the house (group); or the closet (individual solitude). Even though any one of the three places of discernment may be chosen as a starting point, the other two will come into play, either directly (for example, the movement from committees to large assemblies) or indirectly (an individual's attention to the distant voices of faith traditions). All three locations interact to form a dynamic, charged process which is not repeatable; no process of discernment is ever exactly the same as another.

The ten movements are listed across the top of the "Discern-O-Map." The three settings for discernment are listed down the left side of the page. With the map before us, we are ready to plot the route. At each step in the process, put a dot in the appropriate location on the map to indicate where the action takes place. Once you have placed the dots, connect them with a solid line if contact with the assembly, group, or individual is direct and with a dotted line if contact or attentiveness is indirect. Begin the line, which indicates the route of discernment, on the left side of the page under the movement and beside the setting where discernment begins. Then draw the line to the right to indicate where each movement in the process takes place. (The solid line will move back and forth among the three settings for discernment. From time to time, a dotted line may extend from the solid line.)

For instance, if the beginning point for discernment is with the individual and he or she enters into dialogue with a small group of people who offer support, wisdom, and clearness, a dot would be placed under the appropriate step and across from the word *group*. If he or she needs to look to the wisdom of a particular faith tradition that has been expressed through a large assembly, a dot would be placed across from the word *assembly*. A solid line would be drawn from the dot beside *individual* to the dot beside *group*, and a broken line would connect the individual with the assembly.

If a large assembly frames an issue to be discerned, a dot is placed under the framing step and beside *assembly*. If smaller groups are to be invited to participate in the discernment process, another dot is placed beside *group*. A dot is placed at the *individual* level when opportunity is to be afforded for private prayer and reflection.

When we plot spiritual discernment through the ten movements, in the process we will record the actions at the assembly, group, or individual levels. The line will compare to the line on the map, charting a journey. The line on our map of discernment will move horizontally if there is no interaction among the settings. But if there is interaction or attention, the line will oscillate back and forth. Discernment is a changed, dynamic process. We offer this "Discern-O-Map" to the discernmentarian so that she or he can serve as a tour planner and guide.

THREE TRACKS FOR DISCERNMENT

Now let's illustrate an exciting journey into discernment. We will walk with an individual, a group, and an assembly through the ten movements of the discernment process.

INDIVIDUAL DISCERNMENT

Put yourself in the place of an individual who wants to discern God's will, guidance, or call. It is an exciting opportunity, but it is scary as well. There are plenty of reasons to hesitate:

• Discernment moves you to holy ground, the arena of divine presence and will. Holy ground may not be familiar territory; you may be more comfortable doing what you think is best. God's will dramatically changes the equation. So you may be prone to hesitate or resist.

• At an earlier time, you may have been convinced that you were responding to the will of God, and nothing turned out as you expected; you may have ended the experience with second thoughts about whether you followed God's leading.

• Other people may have taken advantage of you by claiming to know God's will and may have tried to impose it on you. Since God's will is a mystery, you wonder if God's yearnings can ever be known by mere humans.

• A final stumbling block to your seeking God's will may be your predisposition to resist the search. Are you willing to follow God's yearning when you know it? You may not want to know God's will, or you may fear that God will ask too much of you or require you to change too much.

Rather than getting stuck in your concerns about negative results, realize that God offers more, and more, and more! God loves you and yearns for what is best for you.

Initially, a wise and skilled discernmentarian can meet with you to map out a course to follow, a process of discernment that will finally bring you to the Spirit's leading.

Step into the shoes of an *individual*, a novice discerner, who desires to know the will of God. Suppose that you have been approached by the chairperson of the church's nominating committee and have been asked to serve a three-year term on the church's board or administrative council. Knowing that several people in the congregation are spiritually wise and have been schooled as discernmentarians, you, the novice discerner, seek out a discernmentarian for assistance. The discernmentarian describes in detail the ten movements to discernment. You work with the discernmentarian to plot a course on the Discern-O-Map that will provide you with two weeks of prayerful and thoughtful consideration of the invitation to serve on the church board. Here is how your Discern-O-Map might look:

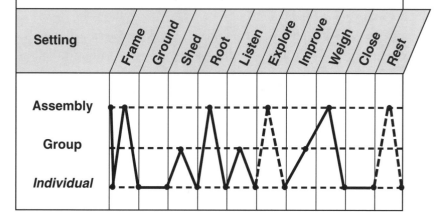

Framing

The invitation from the nominating committee (representing the assembly or congregation) has precipitated the matter to be framed for discernment. For what issue do you seek God's guidance? By framing the issue in a question, "God, are you calling me, through the voice of these people, to serve as a spiritual leader of this congregation?" You now have a clear matter to consider for discernment.

The line on the Discern-O-Map begins with the *assembly* (represented by the nominating committee), moves to a dot across from *individual*, then returns to the level of *assembly* (represented by the discernmentarian), and returns to the level of the *individual*, because the discernmentarian has agreed to guide you. The movement from assembly to individual takes place in the "Frame" stage. Turn to your Discern-O-Chart and record your initial feelings of being unworthy for the task and your initial contact with a discernmentarian.

Grounding

After several days of mulling the matter over, you find that a guiding principle has come to rest in your mind and heart, which is: *"Whatever I am called to do, my gifts and energies should be placed at God's disposal."*

Because the guiding principle came from deep within, the line on the Discern-O-Map is drawn horizontally at the level of individual solitude. The guiding principle can now be written in the appropriate space on the Discern-O-Chart.

Shedding

You, as the novice discerner, decide to talk with three friends. You have been eating breakfast with them once a week; and over time, you have come to trust them. All three are persons of deep faith, but they practice it in different denominations. They ask, "What would you have to give up or lay aside in order to follow God's will in this regard?" The answers come slowly: "Some family time," "fear of being drawn into conflicts that I would rather avoid," "fear of change," "having to attend meetings."

The list of things you would give up can be recorded on the Discern-O-Chart. The line on the Discern-O-Map should move to a dot at the *group* level and back again to *individual* solitude.

Rooting

Knowing that the congregation has deep roots in the denomination, you, as a novice discerner, want to know more about your church's tradition. You contact your pastor and ask her or him to relate the history of lay leadership in your church and denomination. Your pastor wisely offers several scripture readings, tells the story of the unique charism of leadership in the church's heritage, provides you with several instructive books, and offers to support you, regardless of the final outcome of the discernment.

The line on the Discern-O-Map can be drawn at the *assembly* level, which is represented by your pastor, and then back to *individual* solitude. You record on your Discern-O-Chart the surprising new information you have learned about church leadership.

Listening

Since you have been invited to serve in a leadership capacity, you ask particular people in the church some pertinent questions about their expectations of the church and their hopes for what it might become. You also ask several friends about their experience serving on the administrative board. One of them offers to become your prayer partner in the process of discernment. You are reminded that the church is both a human and a divine institution.

You log your impressions on the Discern-O-Chart and continue the line on the Discern-O-Map so that it extends to the *group* level. Though it is not a formal group, the individuals you consulted make up a group. You also make a notation on the chart to indicate that your prayer partner is listening in prayer and silence for the voice of God.

Exploring

By now, the guiding principle has become the basis for much reflection. "Is God calling me to use my gifts only in my family? in a ministry to the homeless to which I am committed? or should I use my gifts in spiritual leadership for the congregation as a whole?" A number of other possibilities surface, but these three dominate your attention.

You record on the Discern-O-Chart your questions along with a comment: "This invitation has caused me to consider my plans in the light of God's will, which is a change for me." The line on the Discern-O-Map continues horizontally, but you add a dotted line to *assembly* after having been moved while singing "Here I Am, Lord" in the church's Sunday worship service.

Improving

Now you are ready for the next step: How can you improve each of your three optional choices (family, the homeless, council) so that they are the best they can be, given your guiding principle? You ask the breakfast group; and they respond, naming and identifying the unique gifts you possess and suggesting possible ways to use your gifts in each situation. They ask a question: "What brings energy and excitement to your life?" Then they promise to continue to pray that God's Spirit will lead you in the path God yearns for you to follow.

You record your gifts on the Discern-O-Chart and draw the line on the Discern-O-Map, which continues to the *group* level. Your breakfast friends have functioned as a "clearness committee."

Weighing

You show the discernmentarian how you have followed your Discern-O-Map, and you read aloud what you have recorded on your Discern-O-Chart. The reading proves to be most enlightening; you begin to see that a direction is emerging. "Let's move ahead," you decide; and you write those words on your Discern-O-Chart.

A dot is located at the *assembly* level on the Discern-O-Map because the discernmentarian represents the church. The line is drawn to the dot and then back to the level of *individual* solitude.

Closing

A combination of intuition, spirit, conviction, and reason lead you to decide that this is the time for you to step into church leadership. By serving in this capacity you can help the congregation share your passion for working with the homeless. You can also set some priorities with your family and make a covenant to give them time and energy so that the time with your family will be quality time.

You record this information on your Discern-O-Chart.

Resting

You call the chairperson of the nominating committee. "Yes," you respond, "I am excitedly looking forward to it. I want to spend some time living with the decision; but if I don't call you back in three days, count me in." Over the next few days, you have a buoyant and positive feeling about the decision. You feel that you entered holy ground, that God has led you. The story of Moses and the burning bush continues to surface in your mind.

In fact, your entry on the chart includes a sketch of a flaming bush with the words *I Am* written under it. The line on your map is spiked to a dot at the *assembly* level, representing your church's tradition. It has offered you a biblical image through the reading which your pastor suggested.

GROUP DISCERNMENT

The small group of three to twelve persons provides the optimum setting for group discernment. (Larger groups may enter into discernment, but the group dynamics are somewhat different.) The group's purpose may be ministry, prayer, or support. Or the group may be a planning committee, church council or board, judicatory staff, or council of the denomination.

Resistance to discernment may be a factor in the primary group, but in different ways than for the individual. Adequate trust may not have been developed within the group. Some people may prefer to keep matters on a rational and impersonal basis: "Just stick to the facts," they may say, "and we will do what we think is best." Others say that discernment takes too much time.

Discernment certainly takes time. The primary group will not choose to submit every decision to an extended discernment process. However, when the group identifies a major issue for discernment, it may devote the necessary time to work toward a conclusion that is in accord with God's leading and has the support of the whole group.

Step into the shoes of a discernmentarian invited to work with a primary group that is about to enter into the process of spiritual discernment. The group is ecumenical and consists of twelve members—both lay and clergy, Catholic and Protestant. They have covenanted to begin a non-profit ecumenical ministry and have secured the services of several staff members. A group of trained consultants also has offered its time and resources to share in the work of the ministry. The group has developed a particular style of leadership development ministry that has the potential to create vital congregational life and mission. You are the designated discernmentarian, chosen to lead the group on its journey through the process of discernment.

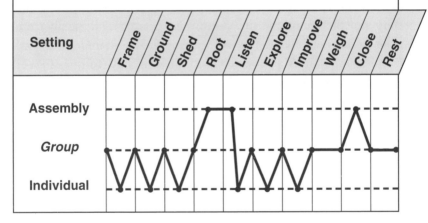

Discern-O-Map

Place a dot at the level where each movement will take place. Then connect the dots with solid lines for formal contact and dotted lines for informal attention.

Setting — Frame / Ground / Shed / Root / Listen / Explore / Improve / Weigh / Close / Rest

Assembly
Group
Individual

Framing

Having introduced the group to the ten movements of discernment, you display a large Discern-O-Map and ten large sheets of paper, with the name of one of the ten movements written at the top of each sheet. You help the group members frame the matter they want to discern. You ask them to tell the story of how the group came into being so that the group begins to form a corporate memory of their own story. Encourage them to name and celebrate each person's gifts and his or her role in the story.

Then you identify the particular style of ministry that is now being called for and invite the group to take a look at the people and events that defined and embodied this particular ministry. The group will recall that it has recently been involved in spiritual leadership development in several test congregations and that its current mission is to spread the word by bringing what it has learned about leadership to more congregations and other religious communities. The discernment issue is being *framed*. The members of the group agree to unite in a common prayer that God will show them how to extend their ministry to 325,000 congregations in the United States so that their insights into spiritual leadership may be helpful to the larger church. You wish to shorten the prayer focus to "God, show us how to spread our ministry to other congregations."

The line on the map, which began at the *group* level, will be drawn to the *individual* level and back to a dot beside *group*. The stories of the group and the stories and gifts of each member are isolated and celebrated. You will write on the chart, under the word *frame*, the group's prayer: "God, show us how to spread our ministry to other congregations."

Grounding

The selection of a guiding principle must be rooted in the values of their faith community. The group is aware of its limited financial resources. It expresses concerns about the health of the staff with high demands for travel and meetings. At the same time, it holds a lofty vision to make an impact on the larger church. The members of the group want other congregations to experience life-giving meetings which are rooted in spiritual practices. You invite each person to enter into an extended silence and then to write a one-sentence statement that could guide the group's discernment.

When the statements are read, look for a common theme to emerge. "We see our work as a living, growing organism rather than a highly promoted administrative organization." Someone says, "Find where the energy lies and go with it." "We recognize the financial limitations and the energy limitations of the staff." "Take time to listen to God in the process." Pulling together their statements, you offer a trial balloon for the guiding principle: "Allow God to grow our efforts, as the Spirit creates opportunities." They like your summary, but they want to add "and wholeness for all" so that the principle takes into consideration the health of the staff.

You record the guiding principle on the chart and draw the line on the map to a dot at the *individual* level and then back to a dot at the *group* level. The time spent in silent prayer and reflection was an essential part of the process.

Shedding

Suggest that the participants work in groups of two or three persons to identify what the group must lay aside in order to be open to the growth God gives. You give each person a portion of clay and invite her or him to create a symbol for each item of baggage that needs to be discarded. When everyone is finished, ask the small groups to place their clay symbols on a centrally located table. Making the symbols will stretch the group beyond familiar and safe patterns. The group might call for a laying aside of financial concerns and place its trust in God to continue to bless what God has started. What if one creative soul re-formed the clay symbols into a single cross while the group sang, "Lord, Have Mercy Upon Us."

The line on the map moves horizontally along the level of the *group*, except for a short extension to a dot beside *assembly*. The cross and the response "Lord, Have Mercy Upon Us" are part of the tradition of the church. Someone could sketch on the chart a representation of the clay symbols and the symbol of the cross over them.

Rooting

Your discernment group has been made aware that the exile of Israel in a foreign land is a powerful image that could be used to describe the situation of the church today; the church is no longer safely harbored in Christendom as perhaps it once was, nor has the church clearly defined its place in the world. "What part of the exile is the church in today?" a participant asks. "Are we entering a period of exile?" "Are we on our way home?" Since this is an ecumenical group, you invite the participants to talk about each of their churches: "What part of the exile is your church in?" An amazing consensus may emerge around the themes of rebuilding. One person catches the imagination of the group by talking about Nehemiah, who returned from a foreign land to rebuild the city of Jerusalem. The participants agree to read the first chapter of the book of Nehemiah that evening. It offers clues to the centrality of vision, prayer, and leadership.

The line on the map is drawn to a dot on the *assembly* level, where it rests. That tradition, which has been passed down from the history of the people of God, will continue to speak to the group in its future gatherings for discernment. The symbols of the spade and the sword can be entered on the chart because workers on the Jerusalem wall worked with a spade in one hand and a sword in the other. (See the book of Nehemiah.) The symbols represent the integration of the work of the day and the work of the Spirit, of ministry and spirituality.

Listening

To prompt the listening step, you ask, "Whose voices do we need to hear now?" They respond, "We need to listen to our founding stories and see how they might speak to us. What can we learn from our failures and our successes? What can we learn from the experience of other ecumenical organizations that have held high vision? They should have plenty to tell us. What are pastors and lay leaders saying about the situation in their churches?" See if individuals in the group will volunteer to make phone inquiries before the next meeting. In the meantime, they make a covenant with one another to pray daily and to listen for the voice of God in the voices of the people with whom they speak.

The line on the map is drawn to the *assembly* level and also to the *individual* level.

Exploring

You play appropriate background music as people settle in, quieten down, and center. Then you ask each person to consider a path that could take the group's leadership experience and insights to the wider church. The participants should consider the questions: Where does the path lead? What will it take for us to walk it? What are the obstacles in the path? What are the helps along the way? When the various pictures are presented, you caution the group to withhold judgment, but to keep in mind the options that seem to welcome or discover God's presence. Then invite each person to reflect on his or her own drawing.

The line on the map is drawn from the *group* level to a dot across from *individual*.

Improving

After each person has described a possible path the group could take, it becomes clear that the paths they suggest can be consolidated into four options: holding theme-focused conferences, consulting with congregations, providing resources, and guiding formation retreats. The line on the map moves horizontally, at the *group* level, to the next dot, then dips to the *individual* solitude level, where it rests. You record the four paths that have been pictured on the chart. You invite the group to work to improve each path to make the best that it can be.

Weighing

You begin the next meeting by asking the group to spend fifteen minutes in silence, during which time each participant pictures the Spirit of God resting on one or more of the suggested paths. Invite them to look for consolation or desolation as they prayerfully consider each option.

Closing

When the group regathers from the quiet solitude, invite them to describe the four options and their feelings generated through their explorations. Ask if they are ready to close or if they need more time to pray, reflect, repeat a step, or probe into an issue more thoroughly. They indicate they are ready to proceed.

The line on the map moves to a dot across from *group* and continues horizontally.

You then invite the group to talk about the path or paths on which it seems the Spirit of God is resting. At this point, you will have some "sense of the meeting," the leading of the Spirit, and will be able to make a final and more thoroughly developed minute. You offer it and test for consensus or for other responses listed in Chapter Four.

Members of the group may want to embrace all four options and to arrange them in order of priority. They could also place limits on one of the paths in order to cause it to lie within the guiding principle. Until a guiding principle has been changed by the group, it should not be violated. The group then celebrates the gift of God's leading and enters into prayer for the staff and the consultants who will be holding theme-focused conferences, consulting or leading congregations, providing resources, and guiding formation retreats.

The line on the map peaks to a dot at the *assembly* level to indicate the group's awareness of potential client churches. Note on the chart that conversations will be initiated with denominational organizations and that the group and the staff will continue to look for selected ways to walk the paths.

Resting

In the final step, ask the participants to rest the decision near their hearts. At the next gathering, you will offer the opportunity for anyone to relate his or her experiences of either consolation or desolation. If many of the group members experience desolation, some of the steps in the process may need to be revisited. Conversations with denominational organizations may have brought new wisdom to the discernment process, causing the issue to need to be reconsidered.

Conclude by asking each person to tell the group what they have learned about the practice of discernment. Ask questions such as these: In what ways was your faith formed or reformed? When were you aware of God's guidance? Which discernment practices were most helpful?

Under "Resting," on the chart, the entry reads, "God's will, nothing more, nothing less, nothing else."

ASSEMBLY DISCERNMENT

Many religious bodies desire to enter into discernment but are too large to experience the intimate interaction that is possible in a small group. These bodies may be congregations, religious communities, denominational judicatories or districts, or national assemblies. Congregational or local judicatory meetings are generally scheduled for one day, whereas regional or national assemblies and conferences last from three to seven days or longer. It is standard practice for planning or legislative committees to prepare for national meetings and then to offer resolutions and recommendations to the larger assembly. Parliamentary rules take over and dictate the process that is followed on the floor of the assembly as each recommendation is considered. After a period of debate, in which the motion may be amended, the recommendation is voted on or tabled.

Meetings are conducted this way because the method is familiar. We have been well schooled in a culture of majority rule and parliamentary procedure. It seems to be an efficient model of conflict management for making decisions in large governing bodies that express varying positions and often include a variety of advocacy groups. The rules keep the meeting moving and bring each issue under consideration to a conclusion. It tends to ensure that someone (the presider) remains in control and can adhere to reasonable rules to handle conflict with order and civility. But a high price is paid in non-support, hurt feelings, the need for damage control (repair), and divisiveness in the church.

In this section, we offer a way for a large assembly with subsystems to enter into a discernment process that draws upon and prayerfully focuses the collective wisdom of the assembly. At the same time it honors the varieties of ways that participants come to express wisdom. A debate format may work well for verbal and assertive people; but not for people whose wisdom comes through quiet reflection, silence, and intuition.

A large assembly with a long agenda cannot consider all the issues brought before it through a process of discernment. *Robert's Rules of Order* are appropriate for many such agenda items. But the body may choose to discern the will of God related to one or two significant matters and may put aside parliamentary procedures in order to engage in prayerful discernment. The discernment process could range over several meetings, even if the assembly meets every year or every two years. Some matters are important enough to warrant whatever time it takes to seek the mind of God.

Often conferences or assemblies reach levels of low morale when facing a big issue in which everyone is vitally interested. There are obvious reasons. Faced with a major issue, the people are rightly concerned about who will serve on the important legislative committees which usually generate the recommendations. Many people want to engage at the center of the action, and they resent having to serve on do-nothing, obscure, or mundane committees. The whole assembly anxiously waits for the latest information from the committee or committees dealing with hot issues, and everyone who is not on one of these committees sits by watching the parade, often with downcast spirits.

Why not select one or two issues and agree to ask the entire assembly to be involved in a process of discernment? That is exactly what we propose.

How would it work? Discernment takes place on three levels:

in the large assembly's plenary, in small discernment groups of twelve to fifteen people, and in the individual's solitude. Each level is distinct and makes unique contributions to discerning God's will. In the context of discernment in an assembly, all three settings are used.

Here is a picture of how the normal pattern for parliamentary procedure operates:

• The individual receives reams of background material to read and study before the assembly convenes. During the meeting, more information is distributed. Participants often feel that keeping up with paperwork is like drinking from a fire hose. A discernment question: Wouldn't things be simplified by stipulating one or two major discernment issues and provide them for their consideration?

• Only one group, a legislative or planning committee, considers each issue. But advocacy groups want to speak to the issues, and the committee may choose to hold open meetings in order to hear various opinions. In the last several years, many committees have chosen to study the Bible and to enter into disciplined prayer about the issues they face. They wish to move beyond the political and legislative models for decision making. But the pressures to get on with business are powerful. Can time be allowed for listening and Bible study?

• The assembly can only consider a matter when a motion has been made. Often an issue is not discussed on the floor of the assembly until the last days or hours of the gathering, and sometimes the pressure to adjourn makes it necessary to meet in the wee hours of the morning. Convincing oratory and reasoned judgment all too often carry the day. Has due consideration been given to God's will? God's call? the Spirit's leading?

We propose a rhythm of decision making that moves from the plenary to the small group or committee, to the individual in solitude, to the group, to the plenary, to the group, to the individual, to the group, to the plenary—etc., etc.—back and forth, turning, probing, speaking, listening, writing, thinking, waiting, symbolizing, imagining, praying, and all the while connecting with the riches of the religious tradition until sight, clarity, light, unity, and consolation emerge. Like a prism that is turned until it fills the room with the color of refracted light, the process of discernment turns an issue until a spiritual leading comes to light. Like a hidden treasure, the will of God is uncovered bit by bit until its form is finally revealed. Like the Shaker dance, the practice of these "simple gifts" will lead us " 'til by turning, turning we come round right."

Here is one way that discernment would work in the context of an assembly. Step into the shoes of the presiding moderator of a deliberative assembly of a major religious body. As you meet with the agenda committee to plan an extended five-day meeting, you are aware of a particular concern that will dominate the attention and the energy of everyone in the gathering. You have an idea: "Let's do only the business that we absolutely have to do and use a major portion of the assembly to allow all participants to focus on this one concern. Perhaps we can use a process of discernment."

In fact, you have heard of a discernmentarian, who has insight and gifts in this area; and you secure permission to ask her or him for guidance. You are excited (and a little scared) at the prospect. You invite the discernmentarian to sit with the agenda planning team at its next meeting.

At that meeting, the discernmentarian takes time to guide the committee to consider the ways the early Christian church gathered to decide major issues (see Acts 15). The discernmentarian then presents the ten movements of spiritual discernment, which incorporate many practices used by the church and described in the book of Acts. Adequate time will be given for some aspects of discernment in the large plenary settings. A considerable amount of time will be spent in small groups of twelve to fifteen people, led by a person who has been trained in the dynamics and practices of discernment. Times for covenants of silence in personal solitude can be arranged within each of the groups so that all will be able to reflect, listen, and pray.

The spirit and enthusiasm of the agenda planning committee is akin to the church in Acts 15:22. "It seems good to the Holy Spirit and to us to do this." So you proceed to lay plans using the map and the chart.

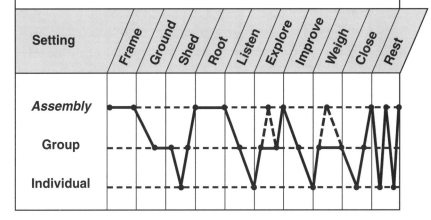

Framing

The matter to be discerned will be framed by the agenda-planning team and presented to the assembly on the first day of the plenary. The team has set clear boundaries for the matter to be discerned and invites the body to search for God's yearning, will, and leading. The assembly's opening worship celebration will lift up the themes of vision, waiting, leading, and calling.

The line on the map can be drawn from a dot beginning at the *group* level (the agenda-planning team) to a dot on the *assembly* level and will then proceed from left to right within the section entitled "Frame."

Grounding

To get the process started, a clear and concise statement of a preliminary guiding principle will be drafted by the agenda team and offered to the plenary. Then the plenary will adjourn, and small groups will meet for a period of at least two hours. The first hour will be used to form community through storytelling and affirmation of the gifts individuals bring to the group. The second hour will be used for three purposes:

- to secure clarity about the subject for discernment that has been framed;
- to finalize a preferred guiding principle which has been offered by the agenda team or to draft a new guiding principle. The feedback will be reported to the agenda team, which will rewrite the statement of the guiding principle, if necessary. It should capture the mind and heart of the whole assembly;
- to come to indifference.

A line on the map will begin at the *assembly* level and move to a dot across from the *group* level.

Shedding

Members of the small discernment groups will be asked to spend some time in silent reflection—then to name the baggage, investments, or passions which each person brings to the issue. They will also be asked to consider what they will have to release so that the group can come to a state of indifference to anything but God's leading. (The group leader will take some time to help the group understand the meaning of indifference.) The participants will also be asked to identify any unique concerns of the religious body they represent in anticipation so that those concerns may be laid aside and the group can come to corporate indifference. The question is this: What needs to die in us individually and collectively so that we can discern God's gifts and leading? The small group session will conclude with prayer. In the next plenary, each group will be invited to offer a prayer during the assembly's worship, as part of confession and repentance.

The line on the map starts with a dot at the *group* level and moves to a dot on the level of *individual* solitude, back to the dot on the *group* level, and then to a dot across from *assembly*.

Rooting

When the assembly reconvenes, the updated guiding principle should be offered to the gathered delegates. If the plenary strongly endorses it, the meeting continues. If not, the agenda team may be asked to rework the guiding principle.

After a period of corporate confession and repentance, the assembly begins to make biblical and historical connections with the matter to be discerned. Several widely respected biblical scholars talk about the themes, images, and stories from the biblical tradition. Such biblical sources pose leading questions for the small groups to consider. A church historian lifts up the historical themes related to the matter and outlines the particular positions of the faith tradition.

A musician or liturgist may invite the assembly to sing verses of hymns that capture the heart of the matter to be discerned. The singing continues until the plenary rests in the mystery of words and harmony.

Under "Rooting," the line on the map moves along the *assembly* level.

Listening

The assembly continues in a plenary session for the purpose of hearing stories. The stories of individuals, congregations, or traditions are not to be made as advocacy speeches. (You, as the moderator, may have to intervene when stories become speeches.) They are to be told in the first person singular or plural: *I* or *We*. In some instances, a small group may choose to tell their story; each person would add to the story by using phrases such as, "and then . . ." or "but before that . . ." The story of how the religious body came to use the process of spiritual discernment may even be an important story to tell!

Then the assembly adjourns so that small groups can meet to discuss the stories which were told in plenary and to continue to explore the tradition. Questions such as these may prompt discussion: Which stories from the plenary session spoke to you? Which connect with your story? What stories in scripture connect with the matter under consideration for discernment? with your story? What do you value and believe because of what you have heard in the stories? What wisdom have you distilled from the stories? The small-group leader will encourage the participants to continue to tell stories and will keep the group from evaluating them or the process too quickly.

A fifteen-minute covenant of silence will be a helpful way for the participants to listen for the voice of the Spirit in the stories. Writing in a journal will arouse a better understanding of the meaning of what they have heard.

Under "Listening," the line on the map begins at the *assembly* level and moves to a dot at the *group* level and then to a dot at the level of *individual* solitude.

Exploring

The discernment groups reconvene and begin exploring the various paths that God may offer. After being introduced to the activity of exploration, the participants are given twenty minutes to work alone and to consider possible options. When everyone has finished, each person presents to the group the possible paths they have considered. Others in the group withhold comment, except for purposes of clarification. At the conclusion, the group's leader or spiritual guide draws a cluster of two to five potential paths related to the discernment issue and names them. Options which the group has suggested are given to the assembly's agenda team; the members of the agenda team will look at all of the possible paths and consolidate them into two to five options for the assembly and groups to consider. The group meeting concludes with an extended period of prayer asking for God's continuing guidance.

The line on the map begins at *individual* solitude and then moves to the *group* level. Under "Exploring," a dotted line is drawn to a dot at the *assembly* level to signify that information has been passed on to them.

Improving

The assembly agenda team identifies a cluster of possible paths and offers them to the small groups for improvement. (If the potential paths do not adequately reflect the work of the discernment groups, this step may begin in plenary for the purposes of ratification. In most cases, however, the assembly does not need to reconvene.) After a brief review of the agenda team's offering, the group members are called to solitude. Each person is asked to prayerfully improve each possible path within the framework of the guiding principle. Then the groups reconvene, and each person is asked to tell how each path can be improved so that each is the best it can be.

Under "Improving," the line on the map is drawn from the *assembly* level to the *group* level, then to *individual* solitude and back to the *group.*

Weighing

The participants remain in the small groups. They are asked to be silent and to allow the Spirit to rest on each path. The questions are posed: Where does the Spirit rest? What path draws us closer to God and leads to consolation? After the silence, the group members report on where the Spirit has led them.

Closing

Because of calendar limitations, the design team has scheduled a closing time. The time was agreed upon in an earlier gathering of the assembly, and it has the weight of an "Order of the Day." Each group leader or spiritual guide tests for consensus or explores various ways to conclude the discernment (see Chapter Four, under

"Closing"). The result and the method or level of response will be reported as information to the agenda team.

Each discernment group has one more task: to select one person who can report to the assembly the wisdom of the group. He or she is a sage, a person who carries spiritual wisdom from the group to the assembly.

When the assembly reconvenes, the agenda team brings to the body a statistical report of the groups' conclusions and the manner or level of their response. It serves as a kind of straw vote. Now the entire assembly can picture the "Sense of the Meeting" as it has been expressed in the small discernment groups. But the discernment is not finished. After an extended time of prayer, a sage from any group may speak to the assembly the wisdom of his or her group. This is not a debate, but a sharing of wisdom; the sage tells the gathered assembly what seemed good to the group as it discerned the yearnings of the Holy Spirit.

As presiding moderator, you may now offer to the assembly several possible ways of concluding the discernment process. You may test for consensus, ask for more time, suggest that people be chosen by the assembly to draw lots, or ask for a vote. Your method of concluding should have the approval of the assembly.

Under "Closing," the line on the map begins at the *individual* level, moves to a dot at the *group* level, and ends at a dot on the *assembly* level.

Resting

You, as moderator of the assembly, record the results of each step on the chart. Then you ask, "How do you feel about the results of our discernment?" Time will tell. God will tell. Suggest that the members of the assembly pay attention to the signs of consolation or desolation. Ask questions: Are you excited about our new direction? Are you taking hold of the vision and beginning to move? Do you have a new sense of hope and vision? Are you acting on our discernment?

You, as moderator, and the agenda team will need to listen closely to the gathered community. Test the waters. Note any negative or tentative responses. The assembly may need to return to some of the prior movements in the discernment process, or the delegates may choose to proceed with boldness and confidence that God is with them.

The line on the map moves back and forth between points on the *assembly*, *group*, and *individual* levels.

⊷ ⬛◆⬛ ⊶

We have now completed the cycle. Please note that there are no hard and fast rules. Bring to discernment your creative gifts, using what we have offered as a starting point. Whether your discernment issue is personal or corporate, in individual solitude, a small group, or an assembly, follow where the Spirit leads you in discerning the will of God.

APPENDIX

ECUMENICAL CHARISM

"Charism" is a gift of God, a spirituality or power unique to a person or group. The charism of a religious group is a gift of the Spirit and may be rooted in its tradition or in its founder. Each religious group brings its own charism to the ecumenical conversation.

THE "CHARISMATA" OF THE TRADITIONS

ANABAPTIST, BRETHREN, MENNONITE, FREE CHURCHES
- The community has priority over the individual.
- There is a constant interplay between the individual and the community.
- God's will is known by responding and doing. Understanding comes in hindsight, and doing involves suffering.
- Discipleship is following Jesus, asking "What would Jesus do?"
- There are no creeds, but listening to the Spirit is paramount.

BAPTIST
- The Scripture is primary.
- Baptist churches function out of the reformed tradition.
- Baptists are committed to evangelism and baptism in the name of Jesus Christ.

UNITED CHURCH OF CHRIST (CONGREGATIONAL)
- The community is the setting for discernment.
- Leaders are called forth out of the community.
- Sermons are a dialogue with the community.
- Councils are called together to focus on opportunities or disputes.

EASTERN ORTHODOX

- Experience is understood within a Trinitarian orientation.
- Doctrines of the Holy Spirit and Scripture are emphasized.
- The Eastern Orthodox Church is suspicious of the doctrine of original sin because of confidence in the Spirit.
- Confession and forgiveness are common practices.
- Liturgical drama includes visualization and the use of images.
- Eastern Orthodoxy has a strong foundation in the traditions of wisdom and mysticism: the places of the Person of Wisdom; the poustinia, a hermitage dwelling on the edge; the living icon; the fathers (abbas) and mothers (ammas) of the desert, who were considered "Holy Fools."

EPISCOPAL

- Scripture, reason, and tradition are sources of authority.
- The Spirit is available to all and enhances listening.
- The Episcopal Church is able to live with ambiguity.

LUTHERAN

- Grace alone, through faith alone and without works of any kind, is sufficient for salvation.
- Scripture and knowledge of the gospel are emphasized.
- The pastor plays a key role in the priesthood of all believers.
- Traditional organization and familiar structures are important.

METHODIST AND WESLEYAN

- The Wesleys brought together divergent strands of faith and action. They linked the devotional life and piety with social justice; mercy and holiness of heart with life; and the individual with the communal.
- The doctrine of sanctification means growing in and through God's grace.
- The conciliar church, unlike a confessional church, seeks the mind of the Spirit in a participating group.
- Wesleyan churches recognize a desire to listen to God; people and the Spirit come together.

- Methodist and Wesleyan churches emphasize the warm heart.
- The will of God is discerned through Scripture, with the aid of reason, tradition, and personal experience—through doing theology.
- Wesleyan churches have a tradition of enthusiasm.
- They practice Christian conferencing, conferring about questions such as these: How is it with your soul? What and how do we preach? teach? How is it with your relationships? with your work or vocation? What should we do? Is there anything you are tempted to keep secret?

NAZARENE
- The focus is on grace.
- Sanctification is a second work of grace.
- God reveals his will, if one seeks and obeys.
- Nazarenes emphasize the disciplines of prayer and fasting.

PENTECOSTAL
- Human experience is a final authority.
- Democratic participation is emphasized.
- Pentecostal churches have a high respect for the Holy Spirit, the third person of Trinity.
- Pentecostal churches minimize the importance of history and tradition.
- Everything is open to the Spirit; special gifts of the Spirit are available for the good of the community.
- Empowered leadership clues the discernment process.
- Marginalized people can influence decision making.
- The sermon is a communal event.
- People are free to express their feelings.
- Signs are evidence of the activity of God's will.

PRESBYTERIAN AND REFORMED
- The church emphasizes both ardor and order and lives in tension between them: The Spirit is active in the work of the church; the

Book of Confessions and the Book of Order guide faith and practice.

- Reliance on God's grace is central.
- The church sees itself as reformed and always reforming.
- Knowing the truth is for the purpose of goodness or righteousness; truth and goodness are connected.
- Scripture is central.
- Historically, the church has committed itself to education.
- The belief that God is sovereign.
- The tradition takes sin seriously.
- Presbyterian and Reformed churches are open to borrowing from other traditions.
- The church is committed to the priesthood of all believers and to the belief that God speaks in community.

FRIENDS (QUAKERS)

- Belief in the witness of the inner light is central; the Spirit speaks to the individual and to the gathered community.
- Friends move toward consensus and beyond; they arrive at the sense of the meeting, when God's will is discerned in the community. They see the need for a Committee on Clearness for individual discernment. They also use a meeting-appointed clearness committee when a person applies for membership or asks to be married under the care of the meeting.
- Silence is an essential practice.
- Friends value peace and reconciliation.
- They rely on group direction and shared leadership.

ROMAN CATHOLIC

- The Roman Church has a long tradition of synods and councils, culminating in Vatican II.
- It is hierarchical in structure and decision making.
- Experience is universal.
- The church listens carefully to the ancient story and recognizes the importance of tradition.

- The charism and the leadership styles of monastic and religious communities, which have practiced discernment, are recognized:
  - Augustinians' discernment through desire;
  - Benedictines' discernment through a patterned life of prayer;
  - Franciscans' and Dominicans' discernment through availability;
  - Jesuits' discernment through what satisfies: savoring the Word of God, drawing on consolation and desolation, listening to details with the head, finding one's heart.
- The church observes seven sacraments. Centered in Baptism, Reconciliation, and the Eucharist, it focuses the calling of baptism and love in abandonment to God's will and in God's call to go and do.

COMMON THREADS FOUND IN THE VARIETY OF TRADITIONS

- Discernment requires the intention to be open to the Spirit and (in a group) to each other.
- Discernment takes time.
- God is present even in the process of discernment.
- The process of discernment forms and deepens communal life.
- Discernment can be surprising; it may not turn out in an expected or predictable way.
- There is risk in entering the process.
- Choices are real.
- There may be more than one right answer.
- The impact of the discernment process extends into subsequent efforts and other aspects of faith and practice.
- God uses gifted and wise individuals for the good of all.
- Adopting the process of discernment moves the culture of the church from win-lose to win-win.
- The need for coming to indifference cannot be neglected.
- There is no place for blame in the process of discernment.
- Confronted with ambiguity, the process goes on.
- Participants should be open to a change of heart.

- An ecumenical dimension broadens awareness of the depth of discernment and offers the gifts of each tradition.
- Growth comes through vulnerability.
- Trust is both a prerequisite and a result of discernment.
- History and story need to be recited and appreciated.
- Freedom to question assumptions is provided.
- The process involves making and uncovering discoveries.
- God is active, so enter the process with fear and trembling.
- There are three different levels of discernment:
  - Is this right?
  - Will we obey? follow the Spirit's leading? count the cost?
  - Will we enter into the presence and mystery of God?
- Discernment leads to involvement with God, with other people, and with the world.
- Discernment flows from and to insight and wisdom.
- Being in the process of discernment means listening for God's voice, God's call, God's promise.

LEADING EDGES

What would happen if we:

- combined Quaker modes of discernment with sacramental practices?
- combined the individual's introversion with a community defined by corporate prayer?
- combined the individual's extroversion with the practice of corporate silence?
- combined biblical or other modes of story-telling with the business agenda of church meetings?
- combined biblical metaphors with church meetings in order to inform the agenda?
- combined broken dreams with new vision?

COMMON WISDOM ESSENTIAL IN DISCERNMENT

- Invitation is powerful.
- Language is important.

- Honest confrontation is possible.
- Religious leaders are gatekeepers.
- People yearn to discern God's will.

REALITY CHECKS FOR THE PRACTICE OF SPIRITUAL DISCERNMENT

- Spiritual discernment takes time.
- The discernment process does not preclude an agenda.
- Some important matters do not need to be discerned, e.g., accepting a report, approval of minutes.
- Other matters can best be determined through discernment by consensus, e.g., is the idea we are considering the will of God?
- Death and resurrection are involved in the discernment process.
- The process calls for mutual vulnerability.
- Turfdom is sublimated. All persons involved must be committed to seek God's will even when it means giving up something.
- If there is no consensus, a prior decision stands or no decision is made.
- It is desirable to identify issues for discernment in advance to allow the group to consider them prayerfully.
- At the beginning of the discernment process each person assumes responsibility for his or her position rather than, "Well, a lot of people are saying . . ."
- The adversarial style of debate is transformed into dialogue and complementary relationships.
- Listening to others takes on greater importance when you are trying to hear the voice of God speaking through them.
- When we gather for discernment, God is with us.
- Discernment involves testing a decision, i.e., what fruits does it produce?

("Reality Checks for the Practice of Spiritual Discernment" is from *Yearning to Know God's Will*, page 108.)

GLOSSARY OF TERMS

A LEADING

In a business meeting, Friends wait in silence for the inner prompting of the spirit and for someone to speak about a leading. A *leading* is what an individual feels that the Holy Spirit, or the Guide, is communicating to his or her inner spirit; a leading of the Spirit is for the benefit of the entire group. Friends share their leadings on the issue at hand, seeking to know God's will for the group. The group's discernment of God's will is expressed through consensus.

Consensus among Friends does not always mean that a process continues until everyone finally agrees. There are times when consensus means that a proposal is reshaped until there is consensus not to block it. For example, a Friend may say, "I am still not totally satisfied, and I cannot enthusiastically support the proposition; but I do not feel required to oppose it in order to be true to my conscience." If anyone does not feel easy with the proposal (minute), his or her reasons are seriously considered.

CONSOLATION AND DESOLATION

More than 400 years ago, St. Ignatius of Loyola produced the Ignatian Spiritual Exercises.[1] Popular forms of the exercises are called "The Thirty Day Silent Retreat," "The Eight Day Silent Retreat," or "The Three Day Silent Retreat." Spiritual discernment and the feelings of consolation and desolation are central to the retreats.

Ignatius said that in spiritual discernment, we do not seek God's will as one of several possibilities. We do not offer God multiple-choice options. Rather, we use conventional methods of decision making and choose the one best possible option from among our choices; then we seek to discern whether our choice is God's will.

Ignatius also said that matters for spiritual discernment are always questions with yes or no answers. So we make our best choice, using inquiry, cognition, and research. Then we offer our choice to God in prayer: "God, is this your will, yes or no?"

Ignatius said that we know the answer to the question, "God, is this your will?" by the feelings we experience. The Holy Spirit responds to our question by giving us feelings of consolation or desolation. Once we have offered our choice to God in prayer, we wait patiently and listen.

Consolation is like peace, freedom, light. Consolation is the joy that comes when we consider the choice we have made. The choice seems right.

Desolation is the opposite. It is a troubled, ill-at-ease feeling, a feeling of heaviness, the absence of peace and joy, darkness. Instead of feeling free, we feel stifled. The choice doesn't feel right.

Feelings of consolation and desolation may occur alternately; but in time, one will become dominant. Either consolation or desolation will, eventually, prevail.

If we experience consolation, we continue to pray about the matter and also begin to talk about it with spiritual friends, saying, "I am experiencing consolation when I pray about a subject of discernment. Do you affirm my feelings?" Consolation should always be checked out thoroughly within the Christian community because it is possible for an individual to be wrong in his or her discernment.

We should ask spiritual friends to consider our experience of desolation too. If the feeling of desolation persists, we may offer another option to God, asking, "Is this your will, yes or no?"

MAJORITY RULE

Robert's Rules of Order is today's best known and most widely used method of parliamentary procedure.[2] It is popular, in part, because it is a logical and straight forward method of dealing with items that come before a deliberative body, and also because many persons have been trained in the method.

One of its strengths is that it is suited to handling differing points of view on a particular subject. Through the skillful use of logical steps, a group can come to the final decision that is most widely approved. However, *Robert's Rules of Order* is an adversarial system of arbitration.

The spiritual discernment and consensus approach is a uniquely different but complementary system. In spiritual discernment, the goal is to seek God's will, rather than the will of the group. The presider and/or the decision-making body can determine when the rules of order should be used and when the practices of spiritual discernment are more appropriate.

In *Robert's Rules of Order*, a vote usually concludes each item of business. For the most part, the majority, fifty-one percent, determines the outcome. Since a majority is the determining factor in *Robert's Rules of Order*, we refer to the entire system as majority rule.

COUNT ONLY THE "YES" VOTES

Members of the First United Methodist Church in Tulsa, Oklahoma, designate times when they only count the *yes* votes.

If the desired action is clearly within the framework of their goals for ministry and if a certain number of people are needed to support the new ministry, not everyone is asked to vote on the matter. The pertinent facts are presented. On this question, only the *yes* votes will be counted. With general agreement, only the people who will be active in the ministry vote on the issue. If twenty people are needed, the *yes* votes are counted to be sure there are at least twenty; and the action is concluded.

Only counting the *yes* votes keeps people from voting on something for other people to actually do.

The guiding principle is this: When the action is clearly within the church's mandate, when a limited number of people will bring the action to life, and when the group agrees, only the *yes* votes should be counted.

A PRISM

Imagine that a group is sitting in a circle. In the center of the circle is a table. Someone places on the table the proposition that your group is considering.

We can now see a major difference between a meeting defined by majority rule and a meeting for the purpose of spiritual discernment? Under majority rule, people in the meeting considering the proposition would debate or argue with one another, each person trying the outdo, overdo, or undo the positions taken by previous speakers.

In a meeting for spiritual discernment, each person considers the proposition and each one speaks (if they wish to), the group reflects in brief periods of silence so that what has been said has time to sink in. As each person speaks, the proposition is changed. Think of the proposition as a prism. Imagine that what each speaker says shifts or turns the prism. As members of the group continue to speak, the proposition is continually reshaped; the prism is repositioned, again and again, until the light hits it just right. When the light of God's truth is revealed, everyone can see it from wherever they are sitting in the circle. "Some issues or questions would require little or no turning. But when an issue needs to be considered from many points of view, we would continue to turn it in the light until the truth was revealed. Then everyone can see it at once. The process of turning an issue might sometimes mean giving up something or adding to or modifying or replacing it altogether."[3]

THE HUDDLE MEETING AND A WISE ONE

In a large deliberative body, the smaller discernment group leaders huddle together to review the progress of the groups, the options they have chosen, and the methods and results of the eventual closing.

In this huddle meeting, each group may be represented by the group leader, and/or the group's sage or selected wise one.

Since participants may not know one another before the first gathering of the groups, the sages should be selected on the final day of group meetings. During the final session, the wise one can prepare to confer with the group leader. A wise one who is selected to serve as a representative of the group is not necessarily the person with the most wisdom (or personal maturity). The selection of the group's representative should be based on his or her participation in the group. In all probability, several participants are qualified to be the wise one. Rather than using time to make the selection or turning the selection process into a popularity contest, the group should choose someone who can speak his or her own wisdom and passion and is willing and able to devote extra time, thought, and prayer to the task.

This person and the group leader confer. They review the full extent of the group's meetings and strive to bring forth an accurate representation of the feeling tone, as well as the specific outcomes, of the process of discernment.

GROUP SIZE

In large deliberative bodies, the optimum size for discernment groups is fifteen, plus the group leader. The preferred size is seven to twelve. The number of groups will be determined in part by the number of meeting spaces available. However, the size of the groups is more important than their privacy or comfort, since the groups will meet briefly (probably two hours a day) and only a few times. In order to keep the groups small, care should be given to making available as many meeting places as possible.

If the time available for group meetings is short, the groups should be smaller. A group of fifteen people will need at least one-and-one-half hours to engage with one another. Groups of seven or eight people may require only forty-five minutes to an hour.

ORDER OF THE DAY

In large deliberative bodies, provision should be made for an Order of the Day so that times for discernment can be listed on the agenda and so that other agenda items do not crowd out the plenary presentations or the meetings of the discernment groups.

GOVERNANCE

Spirituality has had and continues to have a dramatic impact on the church. We saw the influence of spirituality first in worship, then in education, and now we see it entering into governance.

At the turn of this century and into the next century, the church will have to come to terms with how it makes decisions. Perhaps by then, we will have made substantial progress in formulating a new kind of church, in which God's will is valued and sought above all other considerations, and in which the leadership knows how to access practices of the faith tradition for their ordering of its common life and ministry.

PROPOSITION/OPTIONS

When a large deliberative body uses the process of spiritual discernment to consider a major proposition, the members of the body form smaller groups to discern the leading of the Spirit. No one group is free to reframe the proposition because other groups are considering it at the same time.

However, a single proposition may include a number of options. For example, if a deliberative body were deciding to change its name, the proposition should properly list the proposed new name: The XYZ Company. The proposition should not be changed, but it could include options: 1) to keep the previous name or 2) to adopt a new name other than the one proposed.

Any option that is significant to the body may be considered. The proposition and options for consideration should be framed as sharply as possible so that the groups will have the best possible beginning for their process of discernment.

Because the proposition and any approved options may properly become subjects for discernment, the bottom-line question for each is always, "God, is this your will, yes or no?"

MAKING A MINUTE

Friends (Quakers) talk about making a minute (singular) and writing or recording a minute. Making a minute is quite different from taking minutes. The plural form, taking minutes, means keeping up with all the items that come before a decision-making group and recording the actions that are taken. The minutes (plural) become an official record of the meeting. In a Friends Meeting, the plural "minutes" are important enough to be immediately read to ensure that they are accurate.

Making a minute is significantly different from taking minutes. Unlike the secretary who keeps up with everything in the meeting to be sure it is properly recorded, the clerk (discernmentarian) is only interested in "what is happening now." The clerk listens sensitively to all points of discussion and tries to hear a point of clarity about the subject under consideration. As soon as practical, the clerk may attempt to make a minute, which is a summary or a conclusion of what he or she has heard the group say. The clerk then offers the minute for the group's consideration. If the minute seems acceptable to the members of the group, the clerk allows them time to reflect on, discuss (prayerfully), and refine the minute if they choose to do so. I (Danny Morris) have often heard Douglas Steere say, "A well disciplined business meeting permits a space between members' speaking when the substance of what has been said can be considered." When the clerk feels that the time is appropriate, he or she may read the minute. Then he or she will ask, "Does anyone feel uncomfortable about our proceeding in the way I have just stated in the minute?" If no one speaks, it is assumed that consensus has been achieved; and the clerk announces the consensus.

Sometimes consensus cannot be reached because someone in the group cannot, in all good conscience, support the minute. In that case, he or she may request that his or her name be registered in opposition to the proposition. Opposition does not necessarily derail the process or kill the proposition, but it puts the community on notice of a deep concern.

The Friends' provision to honor voices of dissent is an expression of inclusion. When opposition is recorded, the relationship between the individual and the community remains intact; and the conversation can continue. If correction is necessary, the community may attempt to clarify the individual's understanding. Compare the results of an individual's registering his or her opposition with the broken relationships that often occur when, on matters of deep concern, the votes are counted and some people are winners and others are losers.

CONSENSUS/"THE SENSE OF THE MEETING"

Coming to consensus is a way of concluding the consideration of a matter, without taking a vote. Consensus means that everyone is in agreement or comfortable enough to not stand in the way. Consensus does not mean that the opposition has been beaten down, and it does not require that everyone be at the same level of agreement. It may mean that the matter has been so thoroughly considered and subsequently altered by the process of consideration that no one is offended by or opposed to the proposition.

Someone may say, "It is still not what I would choose if I were making the decision alone, but I feel good enough about the decision that I will not block it." Or someone who opposes the proposal may say "I don't favor the decision, but I will stand aside so that the matter can go forward." Another person may feel strongly opposed to the motion: "I do not favor the decision, and I want my name entered into the record as opposed to it." (This should put the entire body on notice of a serious concern that must be given careful attention.) All of these responses to a proposition may rightly be considered as consensus.

However, if someone through prayerful discernment says, "I am absolutely opposed," and offers no qualifications, then consensus has not been achieved. If the person is unwilling to step aside, his or her response stops the process. The sensitive group will heed the negative response and will take additional steps to revisit the process and to work toward consensus, if possible. The lack of consensus brings a halt to the decision making. There are rare exceptions, usually brought on by a very severe outward need for an answer.

Consensus is an exacting, but significant, discipline of discernment of God's will.

There are limitations to consensus; it is not the ultimate indicator that discernment has occurred. Consensus can occur as the result of human striving and have no spiritual overtones. It is usually a desirable and productive goal, but the more profoundly spiritual way of coming to a decision is arriving at what Friends call the "sense of the meeting."

In it the spiritual gift of confirmation of God's will has been discerned. It is not subject to being turned into an exercise in clever management, red tape, or human achievement.

In group process, the term *consensus* simply means unity of opinion or general agreement. In the Quaker tradition, however, consensus expresses the sense of the meeting about how God is leading the community. It is not only human agreement on religious, political, or economic ideas. It is an expression of our understanding of God's wishes for our community and our faithful living.

This discernment process is a fragile one. Consensus as a human endeavor may be open to pressure from skillful management or preconceived opinions. The discerning group must remind itself regularly that it is seeking God's will, not simply human agreement.

The sense of the meeting may be expressed in diverse ways. Sometimes the Spirit of God settles on a group so palpably that those involved in discernment immediately see with clarity what decision they must make. Other times discerners arrive at the group sense of the meeting only through much prayer, sharing of personal leadings, and inward struggle and transformation. God can be at work in as profound a way in this experience as the first.

The sense of the meeting may even take a form that is different from what has previously been expressed; so the meeting is not always a logical progression (we find A, B, and C, which naturally leads to D.) The Spirit may surprise us.

No matter how the discernment unfolds, it is always important to remember that the sense of the meeting is not simply what we think or feel; it is not what we have worked out. Rather, it is what God is saying to us or asking of us.

WHAT'S IN A NAME?

• *What we are to do* is Spiritual Discernment.

The *way* in which we are to *walk* is a *journey to be made* and we call it Spiritual Discernment.

• *How we live* is Prayerful Discernment.

The *life* which we are to *live* is *a prayer to be prayed* and we call it Prayerful Discernment.

ENDNOTES

Introduction
[1] Alasdair MacIntyre, *After Virtue: A Study in Moral Theory*, 2nd ed. (Notre Dame: University of Notre Dame Press, 1984).

Chapter 1 — Discernment: What?
[1] Stephen Bryant, "What Is Spiritual Discernment by Consensus?," *Raising Prayer to a Lifestyle;* Vol. 2, Issue 1 (July–September 1994), 2.

[2] Origen, *On First Principles* (New York: Harper & Row, 1966).

[3] John Cassian, *Conferences* (New York: Paulist Press, 1985) 1:20, 54.

[4] *Ibid.*, 2:3, 62.

[5] *Ibid.*, 1:21, 57.

[6] John Climacus, *The Ladder of Divine Ascent* (New York: Paulist Press, 1982), 114.

[7] *Ibid.*, 229.

[8] Kadloubovsy and Palmer, *Early Fathers from the Philokalia* (London: Faber & Faber, 1954).

[9] Thomas à Kempis, *Of the Imitation of Christ* (New York: Mentor Bock, 1957).

[10] Igantius of Loyola, *Spiritual Exercises and Selected Works* (New York: Paulist Press, 1964).

[11] John Calvin, *Institutes of the Christian Religion* (Philadelphia: Westminster Press, 1960).

[12] *Ibid.*, 4.3.8.

[13] *Ibid.*, 4.3.10.

[14] *Ibid.*, 4.9.1.

[15] *Ibid.*, 4.9.2.

[16] *Ibid.*, 4.9.8.

[17] *Ibid.*, 4.10.27.

[18] *Ibid.*, 4.10.27.

[19] *The Book of Discipline* (The United Methodist Publishing House, 1992), 71.

[20] Henry M. Robert III, *Robert's Rules of Order*, Revised (New York: Morrow Quill Paperbacks, 1979), iv and v.

[21] James Turner Johnson, *Just War Traditions and the Restraint of War* (Princeton University Press, 1981), 62–63, 297–322.

Chapter 2 — Discernment: Why?
[1] Danny E. Morris, *Yearning to Know God's Will* (Grand Rapids: Zondervan, 1991), 9–10.

[2] *Ibid.*, 29.

[3] *Ibid.*, 29–30.

[4] *Ibid.*, 131–32.

5 Coalter, Mulder, and Weeks, *The Organizational Revolution* (Louisville: Westminster/John Knox Press, 1992), 55.

6 *Ibid.*, 65.

7 *Ibid.*, 94.

Chapter 3 — Discernment: Who?

1 Danny E. Morris, *Yearning to Know God's Will* (Grand Rapids: Zondervan, 1991), 45.

2 *Ibid.*, 45–46.

3 Peter Senge, *The Fifth Discipline* (New York: Doubleday, 1990), 246.

Chapter 4 — Discernment: How?

1 Fairhurst and Sarr, *The Art of Framing: Managing the Language of Leadership* (San Francisco: Jossey-Bass Publishers, 1996), 49.

2 James D. Richardson, *Discernment: My Experience on Trinity Cathedral's Vestry*. Unpublished paper (March 1993). Available from Trinity Cathedral Church, 2620 Capitol Ave., Sacramento, CA 95816.

3 Paul D. White, Jr., *Discerning the Will of Christ*. Unpublished paper (March 15, 1990), 3–5. Available from Trinity Cathedral Church, 2620 Capitol Ave., Sacramento, CA 95816.

4 *Ibid.*, 1–2.

5 Peter Senge, *The Fifth Discipline* (New York: Doubleday, 1990) 243–244.

6 *Ibid.*, 245–46.

7 Paul White, *A Model of Church Management Centered Around Discerning the Will of Christ*, 4.

8 Peter Senge, *The Fifth Discipline*, 247.

Glossary of Terms

1 Ignatius of Loyola, *The Spiritual Exercises of St. Ignatius* (New York: Doubleday, 1964).

2 See *Robert's Rules of Order* by Henry M. Robert III (New York: Morrow Quill Paperbacks), 1979.

3 Danny E. Morris, *Yearning to Know God's Will* (Grand Rapids: Zondervan, 1991), 106.

St. Theresa's Prayer:

May today there be peace within.
May you trust God that you are
exactly
where you are meant to be.
May you not forget the infinite
possibilities
that are born of faith.
May you use those gifts that you have
received,
and pass on the love that has been
given to you....
May you be content knowing you are
a child of God....
Let this presence settle into your
bones,
and allow your soul the freedom to
sing, dance,
praise and love.
It is there for each and everyone of
us.

BIBLIOGRAPHY
RESOURCES ON DISCERNMENT

Barry, William A. *Paying Attention to God: Discernment in Prayer.* Notre Dame, Ind.: Ave Maria Press, 1990.

Blackaby, Henry T. and King, Claude V. *Experiencing God: Knowing and Doing the Will of God.* Nashville, Tenn.: Broadman and Holman Publishers, 1994.

Bonhoeffer, Dietrich. *Life Together.* New York: Harper & Row, 1954.

Brenner, Bart L. *Finding God's Will in a Deliberative Body: Communal Spiritual Discernment and Decision-Making.* Detroit, Mich.: Ecumenical Theological Center, 1993.

Calvin, John. *Institutes of the Christian Religion.* Ed. John T. McNeil. Philadelphia: Westminster Press, 1960.

Cassian, John. *Conferences.* Translation and preface by Colm Luibheid. The Classics of Western Spirituality. New York: Paulist Press, 1985.

Climacus, John. *The Ladder of Divine Ascent.* Translation by Colm Luibheid and Norman Russell. The Classics of Western Spirituality. New York: Paulist Press, 1982.

Coalter, Milton J., John M. Mulder and Louis B. Weeks (ed.). *The Organizational Revolution: Presbyterians and American Denominationalism.* Louisville, Ky.: Westminster/John Knox Press, 1992.

Conroy, Maureen. *The Discerning Heart: Discovering a Personal God.* Chicago: Loyola University Press, 1993.

"Discerning the Spirits." *Weavings: A Journal of the Christian Spiritual Life.* Vol. 10, no. 6 (Nov./Dec. 1995).

"Discernment of Spirits." *New Dictionary of Catholic Spirituality.* Collegeville, Minn.: Liturgical Press, 1993.

Fairhurst, Gail T. and Robert A. Sarr. *The Art of Framing: Managing the Language of Leadership.* San Francisco: Jossey-Bass Publishers, 1996.

Farnham, Suzanne, et al. *Listening Hearts: Discerning Call in Community.* Ridgefield, Conn.: Morehouse Publishing, 1993.

————. *Manual for Discussion Leaders [for Listening Hearts].* Harrisburg, Pa.: Morehouse Publishing, 1991.

Fisher, Roger and William Ury with Bruce Patton. *Getting to Yes: Negotiating Agreement without Giving In.* 2nd ed. New York, N.Y.: Penguin Books, 1991.

Freisen, Garry, et al. *Decision Making and the Will of God: A Biblical Alternative to the Traditional View.* Portland, Ore.: Multnomah Press, 1980.

Green, Thomas H., *Weeds among the Wheat, Discernment: Where Prayer and Action Meet.* Notre Dame, Ind.: Ave Maria Press, 1984.

Hawkins, Thomas R. *Building God's People: A Workbook for Empowering Servant Leaders.* Nashville, Tenn.: Discipleship Resources, 1990.

Heifetz, Ronald. *Leadership without Easy Answers.* Cambridge, Mass.: Harvard University Press, 1994.

Ignatius of Loyola. *The Spiritual Exercises of St. Ignatius.* Edited by Robert Gleason. Translated by Anthony Mottola. New York: Doubleday, 1964.

Johnson, Ben Campbell. *To Know God's Will.* Philadelphia, Pa.: Westminster Press, 1987.

Johnson, James Turner. *Just War Traditions and the Restraint of War.* Princeton: Princeton University Press, 1981.

Kadloubovsy, K.E. and G. E. H. Palmer, ed. *Early Fathers from the Philokalia.* London [Eng.]: Faber & Faber, 1954.

Kelsey, Morton. *Dreams: A Way to Listen to God.* New York: Paulist Press, 1978.

MacIntyre, Alasdair, *After Virtue: A Study in Moral Theory.* 2nd ed. Notre Dame, Ind.: University of Notre Dame Press, 1984.

McKibben, Michael. *Orthodox Christian Meetings: Ideas and Principles for Unlocking More of Our God-given Creative Potential in Our Communications and Administration.* Columbus, Ohio: St. Ignatius of Antioch Press, 1990.

McKinney, Mary Benet. *Sharing Wisdom: A Process for Group Decision Making.* Allen, Tex.: Tabor Publishing, 1987.

Morris, Danny E. *Yearning to Know God's Will: A Workbook for Discerning God's Guidance for Your Life.* Grand Rapids, Mich.: Zondervan, 1991.

Morseth, Ellen. *Call to Leadership: Transforming the Local Church, Parish Council Formation/Education Session.* Kansas City, Mo.: Sheed and Ward, 1993.

Olsen, Charles M. *Transforming Church Boards into Communities of Spiritual Leaders.* Bethesda, Md.: Alban Institue, 1995.

Origen, *On First Principles: Being Koetschau's Text of the De Principiis.* Translated by G. W. Butterworth. Torchbook ed. New York.: Harper & Row, 1966; reprint, Gloucester, Mass.: Peter Smith, 1973.

Presbyterian Church (U.S.A.). *The Nature of the Church and the Practice of Governance.* Approved by 205th General Assembly (1993).

Presbyterian Church (U.S.A.). *Growing in the Life of Christian Faith.* Approved by 201st General Assembly (1989).

Richardson, James D. "Discernment: My Experience on Trinity Cathedral's Vestry" in *The Missionary,* March 1993.

Robert, Henry M., III. *Robert's Rules of Order,* Revised. New York: Morrow Quill Paperbacks, 1979.

Senge, Peter M. *The Fifth Discipline: The Art and Practice of the Learning Organization.* New York: Doubleday, 1990.

———, et al., *The Fifth Discipline Fieldbook: Strategies and Tools for Building a Learning Organization.* New York, N.Y.: Doubleday, 1994.

The Book of Discipline. The United Methodist Publishing House (1992).

Thomas à Kempis. *Of the Imitation of Christ: The Classic Guide to the Spiritual and Moral Life.* New York: New American Library, 1957.

Wheatley, Margaret J. *Leadership and the New Science: Learning about Organization from an Orderly Universe.* San Francisco: Berrett-Koehler Publishers, Inc., 1992.

White, Paul D. Jr. "A Model of Church Management Centered around Discerning the Will of Christ." Paper prepared for Field Education (class) at The Church Divinity School of the Pacific, March 15, 1990.

Wicks, Robert J. *Handbook of Spirituality for Ministers.* New York: Paulist Press, 1995.

Williams, Benjamin D. and Michael T. McKibben. *Oriented Leadership: Why All Christians Need It.* Wayne, N.J.: Orthodox Christian Publications Center, 1994.

Wood, Charles M. *Vision and Discernment: An Orientation in Theological Study.* Scholars Press Studies in Religious and Theological Scholarship. Atlanta: Scholars Press, 1985.